THE LIBRARY OF HOLOCAUST TESTIMONIES

To Forgive…
But Not Forget
Maja's Story

The Library of Holocaust Testimonies

Editors: Antony Polonsky, Martin Gilbert CBE, Aubrey Newman, Raphael F. Scharf, Ben Helfgott MBE

Under the auspices of the Yad Vashem Committee of the Board of Deputies of British Jews and the Centre for Holocaust Studies, University of Leicester

My Lost World by Sara Rosen
From Dachau to Dunkirk by Fred Pelican
Breathe Deeply, My Son by Henry Wermuth
My Private War by Jacob Gerstenfeld-Maltiel
A Cat Called Adolf by Trude Levi
An End to Childhood by Miriam Akavia
A Child Alone by Martha Blend
The Children Accuse by Maria Hochberg-Marianska and Noe Gruss
I Light a Candle by Gena Turgel
My Heart in a Suitcase by Anne L. Fox
Memoirs from Occupied Warsaw, 1942–1945 by Helena Szereszewska
Have You Seen My Little Sister? by Janina Fischler-Martinho
Surviving the Nazis, Exile and Siberia by Edith Sekules
Out of the Ghetto by Jack Klajman with Ed Klajman
From Thessaloniki to Auschwitz and Back by Erika Myriam Kounio Amariglio
Translated by Theresa Sundt
I Was No. 20832 at Auschwitz by Eva Tichauer
Translated by Colette Lévy and Nicki Rensten
My Child is Back! by Ursula Pawel
Wartime Experiences in Lithuania by Rivka Lozansky Bogomolnaya
Translated by Miriam Beckerman
Who Are You, Mr Grymek? by Natan Gross
Translated by William Brand
A Life Sentence of Memories by Issy Hahn, Foreword by Theo Richmond
An Englishman at Auschwitz by Leon Greenman
For Love of Life by Leah Iglinsky-Goodman
No Place to Run: A True Story by Tim Shortridge and Michael D. Frounfelter
A Little House on Mount Carmel by Alexandre Blumstein
From Germany to England Via the Kindertransports by Peter Prager
By a Twist of History: The Three Lives of a Polish Jew by Mietek Sieradzki
The Jews of Poznań by Zbigniew Pakula
Lessons in Fear by Henryk Vogler

To Forgive...
But Not Forget

Maja's Story

MAJA ABRAMOWITCH

VALLENTINE MITCHELL
LONDON • PORTLAND, OR

First Published in 2002 in Great Britain by
VALLENTINE MITCHELL
Crown House, 47 Chase Side
Southgate, London N14 5BP

and in the United States of America by
VALLENTINE MITCHELL
c/o ISBS, 5824 N. E. Hassalo Street
Portland, Oregon 97213-3644

Website: http://www.vmbooks.com

Copyright © 2002 M. Abramowitch

British Library Cataloguing in Publication Data

Abramowitch, Maja
 To Live is to forgive but not forget. – (The library of Holocaust testimonies)
 1. Abramowitch, Maja 2. Jews – Latvia – Biography
 3. Holocaust, Jewish (1939–1945) – Personal narratives, Latvian
 I.Title
 940.5'318'092

ISBN 0-8530-3432-X

Library of Congress Cataloging-in-Publication Data

A catalog record for this book is available from the Library of Congress

All rights reserved. No part of this publication may be reproduced, stored in or introduced into a retrieval system or transmitted in any form or by any means, electronic, mechanical, photocopying, recording or otherwise, without the prior written permission of the publisher of this book.

Typeset in Great Britain by FiSH Books, London.
Printed in Great Britain by MPG Books Ltd, Bodmin, Cornwall

This book is dedicated to my late father, David Zarch; and to my mother, Rebecca Zarch, who passed away on 3 December 1995 aged 98 years. She is one of the unsung heroines of the Holocaust. She saved my life as well as many others through her incredible foresight, wisdom and bravery. The tolerance and compassion she displayed throughout her life was an inspiration to all those with whom she came into contact.

In these pages I am about to recall the truth, and nothing but the truth, in spite of those who labour so maliciously to deny it.

Contents

List of Illustrations	viii
List of Maps	x
Acknowledgements	xi
The Library of Holocaust Testimonies *by Sir Martin Gilbert*	xiii
Introduction *by Gilbert Herbert*	xviii
Foreword *by Sir Martin Gilbert*	xv
Preface *by Maja Abramovitch*	xix
Early Life in Dvinsk (Daugavpils)	1
The Second World War	17
The Ghetto	31
The Citadel	51
Riga–Kaiserwald	60
Stutthof	67
Sophienwald	70
The Walk, Gottendorf and Liberation	75
Freedom and Flight	81
South Africa	106
An Ultimate Pilgrimage	112
A Daughter's Comment	124
Reverie	127
Postscript *by Dr Jack Penn*	128
Epilogue	129
Appendix 1: Footnotes of History	131
Appendix 2: Monuments	134
Glossary	135

List of Illustrations

Between pages 46 and 47

1. Maja's Russian school in Dvinsk.
2. Hebrew school class, taken in 1938. Only three pupils (marked) survived the Holocaust.
3. Picture taken at Maja's birthday party in 1939. Maja is standing top left next to her cousin, Masha Zarch and her second cousin, Rosa Magid, both of whom were killed. Bottom left is Maja's best friend, Eta Maurin; who was sent to Siberia in 1940.
4. Petronella Vilmans, Maja's devout Catholic Nanny, taken in 1956. She is honoured at Yad-Vashem, in Israel, as a righteous Gentile.
5. Mr and Mrs Zarch and Maja, 1936.
6. Riga street, Daugavpils, taken in 1992. The corner shop with the large window was one of Mr Zarch's shops before being nationalized by the Russian government.
7. A synagogue in Daugavpils where Mr Zarch worshipped; it was here that all the Jews were brought together to be killed.
8. The Citadel. On the right of the picture is the building where Maja and her mother lived.
9. The Citadel workshop.
10. Abe Kotzen, a Russian Jewish soldier who warned Maja and her mother not to return to Latvia. Thanks to his assistance they escaped from the Russian zone to the American zone.
11. A group of camp survivors who worked for the Russian Army in Koshalin in 1945–46. Maja's mother is on the far left of the group, and Maja is second from the right.
12. Maja's marriage to Sidney Abramovitch in 1950. Left to right: uncles David and Leon; Maja's mother; Maja;

List of Illustrations

Sidney; Sidney's parents, Ethel and Eias Abramovitch; and David's wife, Lola.
13. Breakfast in Riga with friends. Left to right: daughters Karen and Diana; Mulia Slov (who met the Abramovitch's in Petersburg, and last saw Maja in 1937); Maja; and Sioma Spungin.
14. My family. *Left to right*: son Roy; daughter Karen; niece Shelley; daughter Diana; nephew Martin. *Bottom row*: husband Sidney; son David; and Maja 1998.
15. Memoria Day in Pagulianka Forest where the Jews from Daugavpils were murdered.
16. Granddaughter Kim Smullen at a memorial service at the Johannesburg Cemetary in memory of the victims of the Holocaust.

List of Maps

Between pages xiii and xv

1. Daugavpils.
2. Slave labour camp evacuations, 25 September 1944.

Acknowledgements

This book was written twice. Thirty years ago I wrote a memoir meant only for my children so that they should know. Then two decades later, on the urging of many friends and colleagues, I turned the memoir into a book. Over these years my research led me to a few who survived of the many that died with the rest of my family. They enabled me to fill in most of the gaps in my story.

It is to these and many others who gave their time to enable me to create a personal but authentic record of those terrible times that I render an intense thank you.

I especially wish to thank the following: Peter Buwalda, erstwhile Netherlands Ambassador in Moscow for his kind efforts; Alexandra Levin, herself an author, who insisted that the book should be published; Louis and Lilian Avrutic in Washington for their friendship and persistence that did so much to convert a simple narrative into something more meaningful.

I am indebted to Dr Michael Berenbaum, Professor Gilbert Herbert and Mr Franz Auerbach for their invaluable improvements and to the late Dr Jack Penn who initially set me on the road as a chronicler.

Thanks to Judith Barnes who helped so much when my story first took shape and to Mavis King and Elizabeth Krisch who typed the first and second draughts of the book.

I owe thanks to my publisher Frank Cass and to Georgina Clark-Mazo and Anna Whiston, his dedicated and so-helpful lieutenants.

To Sara Sarkina-Rosenberg I owe thanks for supplying the photographs from our ballet school. To Gessel Maimin I owe thanks for information about historic Daugavpils and last but not least to Sioma Spungin for being such an efficient contact man with the Daugavpils community.

Finally, to my daughters Diana and Karen, who so lovingly held my hand and shielded me during the many overwhelming moments of our trip to Latvia and the harrowing past. To my husband, of course, I find it difficult to adequately express my gratitude. He wrote and rewrote when I no longer could and researched diligently when I did not know how.

It often seems that because I am alive and ultimately blessed, my most intense thanks go to the entire world and its Creator.

The Library of Holocaust Testimonies

It is greatly to the credit of Frank Cass that this series of survivors' testimonies is being published in Britain. The need for such a series has long been apparent here, where many survivors made their homes.

Since the end of the war in 1945 the terrible events of the Nazi destruction of European Jewry have cast a pall over our time. Six million Jews were murdered within a short period; the few survivors have had to carry in their memories whatever remains of the knowledge of Jewish life in more than a dozen countries, in several thousand towns, in tens of thousands of villages and in innumerable families. The precious gift of recollection has been the sole memorial for millions of people whose lives were suddenly and brutally cut off.

For many years, individual survivors have published their testimonies. But many more have been reluctant to do so, often because they could not believe that they would find a publisher for their efforts.

In my own work over the past two decades, I have been approached by many survivors who had set down their memories in writing, but who did not know how to have them published. I realized what a considerable emotional strain the writing down of such hellish memories had been. I also realized, as I read many dozens of such accounts, how important each account was, in its own way, in recounting aspects of the story that had not been told before, and adding to our understanding of the wide range of human suffering, struggle and aspiration.

With so many people and so many places involved, including many hundreds of camps, it was inevitable that the historians and students of the Holocaust should find it difficult at times to grasp the scale and range of the events.

To Forgive... But Not Forget

The publication of memoirs is therefore an indispensable part of the extension of knowledge, and of public awareness of the crimes that had been committed against a whole people.

Sir Martin Gilbert
Merton College, Oxford

Introduction

Historians looking at the Holocaust inevitably take the broad view, attempting to see the whole picture, putting the catastrophe into context. They analyse the mechanisms and logistics of the destruction of European Jewry, they delve into the pathological behaviour of the Nazis in particular and the German people as a whole, and search in history, economics, psychology, for causes, both remote and immediate, which might make sense of the senseless and explain the inexplicable. Philosophers look at the *Shoah*, and try to extrapolate from it universal truths: that prejudice, intolerance and racism inevitably lead to a corruption of morality, a perversion of justice and a denial of the innate humanity of man. In so doing, they sometimes look for analogies in history and draw comparisons with other disastrous events. Their aim of trying to raise the threshold of our awareness to the dangers of intolerance is praiseworthy, but by false analogies and too-facile comparisons they generalize the Holocaust, blur its tragic uniqueness, and diminish the memory of its six million victims. Seen from the outside, as it were, by historians, philosophers, political and social scientists, the Holocaust must be recognized for what it really is, a totally unique historic event.

But in addition to the holistic vision, seeking totality, there are other ways of looking at the tragedy of those years, and that is from within, through the eyes of those who actually experienced it at first hand. After years of reticence, when the pain of memory blunted the ability to speak, there has gradually emerged a literature of remembrance, in the testimony of the survivors. While these testaments deal with a common matrix of suffering, each nevertheless recounts experiences that are totally unique, because they are seen from an individual viewpoint.

They describe the external, objective reality, but in so doing they open up a window into their own souls, as they explore the depth of their own emotions, and probe their own reactions. It was Viktor Frankel who said that while we often have no control over what happens to us, we do have the choice of how to respond. Accounts by survivors of their personal experiences during the Holocaust reveal in the most painful detail the endless cruelties, deprivations and degradations inflicted upon innocent victims of the Nazi terror, a process over which they had absolutely no control. Such accounts also reveal the manner of their response to the ongoing horrors which they were forced to endure, day after day, month after month, year after long year. Maja Abramovitch's story, presented here in her characteristic understated way, gives us not only a close-up picture of the dark side of man's soul, but also an insight into the unquenchable spark of hope when all seems utterly hopeless, which illuminates the human spirit and contributes to the chances of survival in the most desperate of situations.

In these painful memoirs we have a tale of survival against all odds, but not of survival at any cost. The fiendish anti-Semitic onslaught of the Nazis and their many willing allies in Germany, in Maja's homeland in Latvia, indeed throughout occupied Europe, left few Jews who went through the camps alive, and none unscathed. In these circumstances to have survived at all was miraculous, but the greatest miracle of all was eventual survival as a human – a humane – being. In order to survive, providence must be on your side, and fortune, if not exactly smiling upon you, must at least not desert you altogether; good luck is a necessary condition but not sufficient cause for survival. The body must be capable somehow of enduring the endless physical assaults afflicted upon it; the mind must not crack under the unmitigated burden of stress and fear, living from hour to hour on the razor's edge of extinction; and the will to live, the instinct of self-preservation, must be inextinguishable.

Most of all survival demands courage. Courage has many faces. There are single acts of great heroism, the kind which earn medals on the battlefield, or which found expression in brave acts of defiance in the ghettos and the camps. But there

Introduction

is another kind of courage, and that is the courage to endure, to pick oneself up over and over again, the courage to know fear but not succumb to it, the courage not to give in, the courage to go on living, from minute to dreadful minute, when the knowing mind sees no light at the end of the tunnel, but the small flame of hope in the human spirit continues to flicker.

Maja's story of her experiences as a young girl during the Holocaust is a chronicle of courage and survival. The way in which she emerged from the flames, seared in body and mind, yet despite all managed to reconstruct her life, and shape it so positively, is a testament to her strength of character and deep humanity. Her book must be seen especially as a tribute to the memory of a remarkable woman of indomitable spirit, her mother, who even at the darkest hours was always at her side, to plan, give support, to encourage and shield her. It has been my privilege to have known Maja's mother, and to have had Maja's friendship over the many decades since fate brought her to South Africa. Her personal story is important, not only for the insights it provides into human behaviour under stress, but because it expands our general understanding of an opaque and most bitter chapter in the history of the Jewish people.

Professor Gilbert Herbert
Haifa
8 March 2001

Foreword

What Gilbert Herbert has written above is surely right. Maja Abramowitch has written a most important addition to the memoirs of the Holocaust. When she and I met in South Africa 16 years ago, I was struck during our conversations by the powerful nature of her testimony. It is good that she has set down what are often painful recollections, for the benefit of a new generation of Jews and non-Jews, for whom the Holocaust period is 60 years in the past – as far away as were the Tsarist pogroms of the 1880s for those of my generation.

The fate of the Jews of Dvinsk does not figure in many Holocaust histories. It was for that very reason that I had been eager to hear what Maja Abramowitch had to say during my long-ago visit to South Africa. Her account of her childhood there, before catastrophe struck, is itself an important contribution to our knowledge of Jewish history: to our ability to picture the life of pre-war Jewry. It is her story that is important: the comments of the Foreword and the introductions are merely to urge the reader to enter the book itself, and to meet the reality of the Jewish past through the eyes of a remarkable eyewitness.

Sir Martin Gilbert

Preface

Some survivors of the Holocaust cannot bear to read or hear about this period. I have always been interested in reading about it, to see whether it is really impossible to find words to describe adequately the behaviour of the people – the heroism and the bestiality.

It may sound strange. But on meeting some of my co-inmates and discussing with them our sojourn in the camps, it is always the incidents I have described which stand out in their minds as well. Often, wanting to cross-examine myself, I would ask one or another of my intimate friends to tell me of their recollections. Every time I received a letter or a tape, the same 'highlights' would be mentioned.

Human emotions were taxed to their utmost degree. On looking back, I think memory touches the peaks of emotional experience, like a telephone wire stretching from pole to pole without touching what lies beneath them.

There may have been brighter moments to ghetto and camp life, but they certainly evaded me, a child of twelve at the time. I recall only the incidents which made a deep impression on me then, and are still with me to this day.

After the Liberation, when I was 16 years old, other stories I heard about the camps were pale reflections of my own experience. At the time of my arrival in South Africa in 1947, and even before that, people encouraged me to write about my experiences, but it became evident to me that no matter how eloquent I might be, it would be humanly impossible to put these experiences into written words and convey to the reader the full impact of the atmosphere and the sufferings to which we were exposed. Because of this, many valuable records of personal experiences may be lost to the following generation. Even today, long after the event, reading of such things affects me deeply. The wounds have scarred over to a certain extent, but through the words of others, the wounds reopen painfully.

Some years ago, I had to be interviewed by three psychiatrists before I could be granted reparations. One of them, a Dutch psychiatrist, made a statement that interested me. He said that the experience of treatment for my recurrent nightmares would be more painful than the symptoms. The psychiatric world had come to realize the searing effects on the psyches of those who went through the Holocaust.

I spent four of my young, formative years under the most inhuman conditions. I have emerged, I think, a much better and more understanding person. I can put myself into situations that the average person cannot understand – the situation of the poor, the prisoner and the underdog – because I have experienced all these situations. I do not carry a conscious hatred for the nation that subjected me to these conditions, but I cannot deny that in my heart there will always remain a simmering, inexplicable feeling at the mention of that race.

Nothing positive can come from harbouring hatred, but the world would do well to remember the depths of depravity to which nations can descend. Elie Wiesel, the foremost Jewish writer on the Holocaust, maintains that such a thing could not happen in a Jewish state as the Jewish religion has built-in censures to prevent such occurrences. Whatever the case for this may be, I write of my experiences in the hope that they may lend weight to a deterrent preventing a recurrence of such world madness.

Much has been written about the Holocaust, and, until recently, I was not sure whether to heed my friends' insistence that I should commit my experiences to paper. However, an incident occurred some time ago that made me realize how little the past epoch touched some Jews. After a pleasant dinner party in the company of intelligent and erudite people, a respected person stated that perhaps it was time we Jews stopped announcing, at the slightest opportunity, that six million of our people had perished at the hands of the Germans. In fact, eleven million people were eliminated, of whom five million were non-Jews. Perhaps, he said, it was time to stop emphasizing the Jewish deaths and start

Preface

integrating ourselves by looking at the overall picture, forgetting that we are the chosen people. Most of the guests questioned his approach. I was the only person present who had been through the Holocaust and, at that moment, felt more than ever affected by the magnitude of the Jewish annihilation.

No other peoples had remotely approached having over one-third of their numbers wiped out globally, or 70 per cent of those living in Europe, as did the Jews. Yet a Jewish leader had failed to understand the enormity of that disaster. The wilful murder of people – eleven million or six million is relatively immaterial – cannot be condoned even by the glib tendency to say that it was war and war takes its toll in one way or another.

When discussing the Holocaust and the camps, mention is often made about all the non-Jewish people that were also there. I am not denying that they suffered as much as the Jews, but do not overlook one major difference. The non-Jewish people, almost without exception, were put there because they were suspected of being political – anti-Nazis – or because they had committed some other crime. It was only Jews and Gypsies who were there, and killed, because of their race. There is another important difference that is often overlooked. When liberation came, the non-Jewish inmates had homes, country and relatives waiting for them, but the Jews had none of these and nobody cared enough to offer them asylum. This book is written not only as a chronicle of events that should not be forgotten, but as a reminder that it was *people*, often whole families, who suffered and died.

My story begins at a time when most little girls are putting aside dolls and other toys and standing on the threshold of their womanhood, eager for experiences that 'growing up' would bring. But I found myself thrown into a new, horrifying world of war. It was a world where I was perplexed, frightened, and at all times fearful for my life. Fate had decreed that I would become part of the horror to be known as the Holocaust and almost inevitable death.

The term 'Holocaust' refers to the systematic attempt to murder European Jewry that began with the German invasion of Poland and only ended with the capitulation of Germany at the end of the Second World War. By that time over six million Jews had been exterminated out of a total Jewish population in Europe of approximately 9.5 million.

The Holocaust was to have such an effect on the survivors that they did not talk or write about it for many years thereafter. The pain had so deeply scarred their psyche that the memory was locked away and in many cases never resurrected. It was only when the recurring nightmares became too much to bear for me that an outlet had to be found to release the demons within.

Because it was the Second World War and the terrible events leading up to it that made the Holocaust possible, I have decided to include the briefest of what I refer to as 'Footnotes of History' as a backdrop to my story. I felt that the reader might more easily identify with what took place if the great events of the times were interwoven with the horror of the countless individual agonies that form the Holocaust.

What follows is my story, the story of this time of my life that still affects my waking hours and probably always will.

Maja Abramowitch

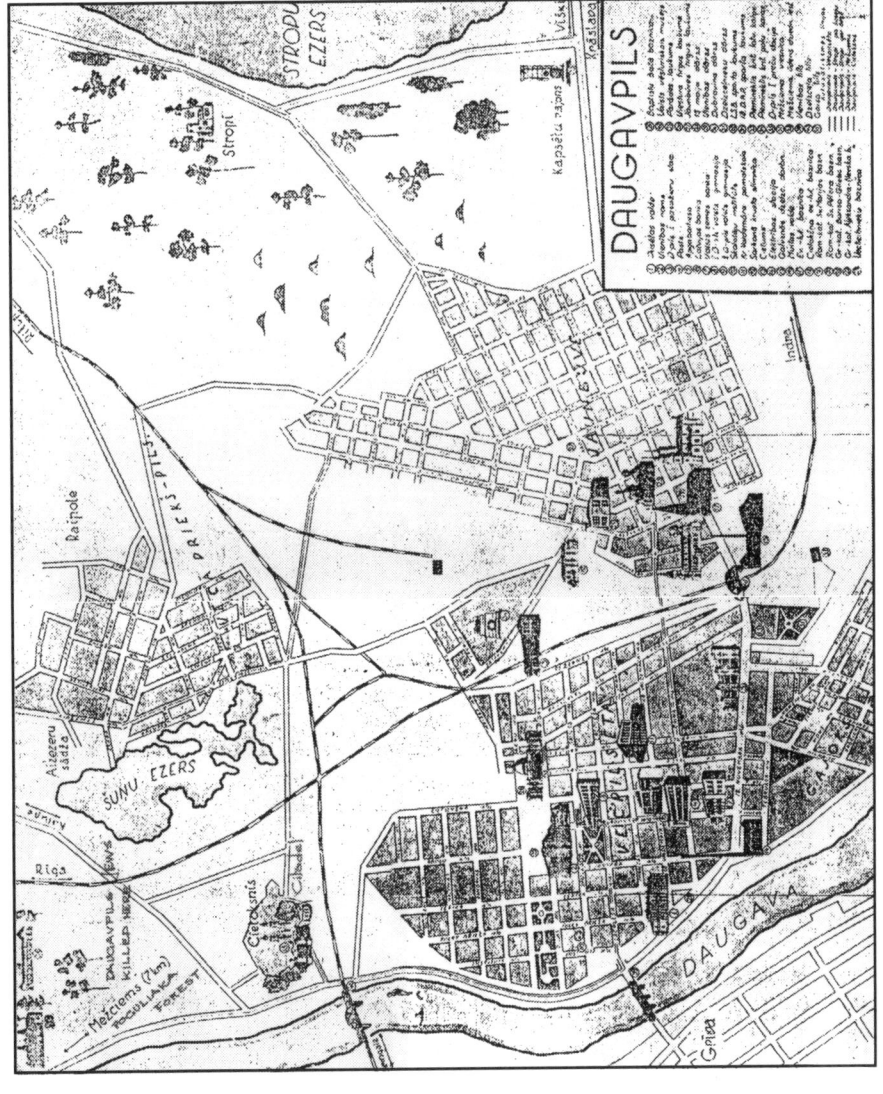

1. Daugavpils.

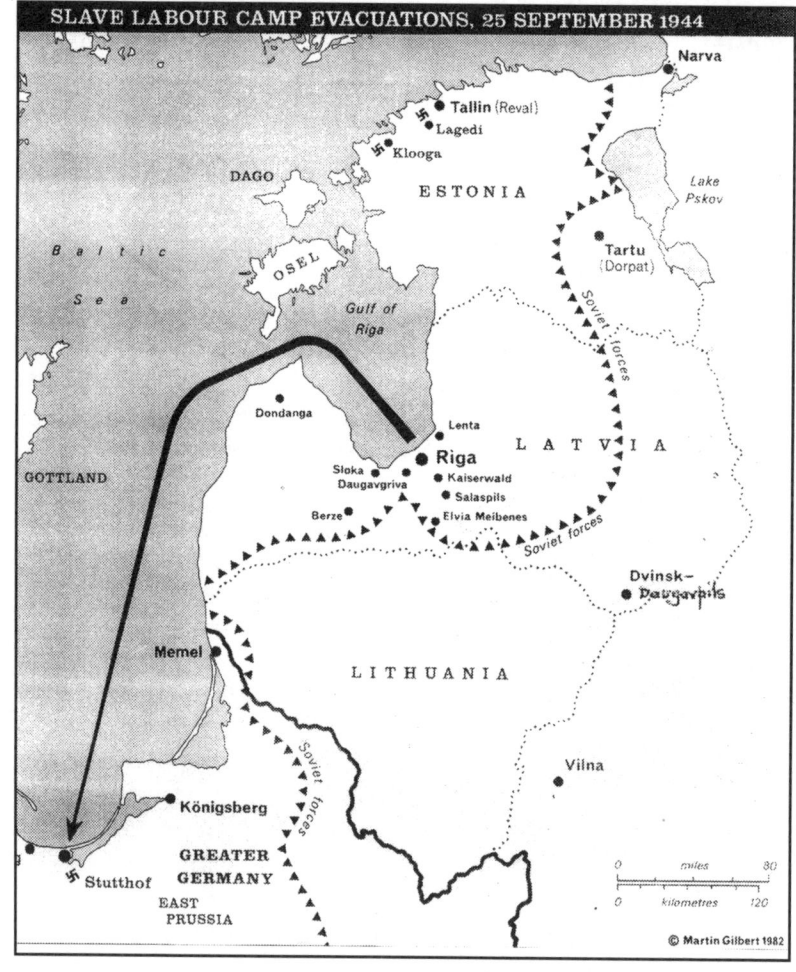

2. Slave labour camp evacuations, 25 September 1944.
[Taken from Sir Martin Gilbert, *Atlas of the Holocaust*, 2nd Edn, Routledge/William Morrow, 1993.]

Early Life in Dvinsk (Daugavpils)

As luck would have it I was born in Dvinsk, now called Daugavpils, on 1 May 1929. This town was an important centre in Latvia, one of the three countries situated on the eastern shore of the Baltic Sea between Poland and the Gulf of Finland. The town's history, reflecting the general history of the country, is one of bloody conquest and frequent destruction.

The Latvians are descended from an ancient people who settled the area about 1500 BC. Because of its central location on the Baltic, the country was traversed by vital trade routes to the north, south and west. Latvia was first conquered – by the Teutonic Knights – in the sixteenth century. Sixty years later it was captured by the Poles; and a century later it fell to the Russians. During the Great War it was the scene of fierce battles between the invading Germans and Russians. In 1918, the Latvian nationalists prevailed and it became an independent country. In 1940, the Soviets annexed it by agreement with the Germans, following the signing of a non-aggression pact between the two erstwhile enemies.

Our family had been established in Dvinsk for many years. For over half a century two prominent shops in Riga Street displayed a very large sign which read: 'Zarch and Sons'. These shops were established by my grandfather Aaron, who first started a business in a small village as a mineral water manufacturer in the latter half of the nineteenth century. Being a man of some education and great natural intelligence, the business flourished. He then decided to move to Dvinsk in 1903 to establish a store that he believed would create greater opportunities for advancement.

My early recollections of him go back to seeing him sitting in front of a Gothic looking box – the radio. He would spend hours on end with his head almost in it, listening to whatever was being transmitted. Our personal contact consisted mainly of my being rather painfully pinched on the cheek by his large thumb and third finger. I realize that this was his way of showing affection but the result was that I avoided any contact with him. On holidays, particularly Hanukkah (the biblical Festival of Lights), in addition to receiving a pinch on the cheek, my cousins and I would receive a handful of coppers with strict instructions to spend them as soon as possible. I immediately put mine into a solid moneybox that was heavy even without the coppers inside. It always gave me a thrill to go to the bank with my father to have the moneybox opened and the money counted. The complicated mechanism of the lock fascinated me and I was constantly puzzled by the fact that however much I tried to shake out the coins through the long slot on top, I could not extricate a single one. This moneybox was kept in the bottom drawer of my parents' bedroom dresser, for maximum safety.

Grandfather lived to the age of 90 and, despite failing eyesight, loved things cultural and attended concerts, to the family's great disapproval. He was a widower with one son, but he later remarried and had a daughter and two more sons. The son of the first marriage went to Russia and the family had little subsequent contact with him.

Father, the younger of the additional sons, attended the commercial school in Dvinsk where he won a gold medal on graduating. He was sent to university in Toulouse, France, to study engineering, but in 1914 whilst he was home on vacation, the First World War started, and he continued his studies at the St Petersburg Polytechnic. The Russian Revolution broke out in 1917 in St Petersburg, leading to my father returning home to Dvinsk.

When Latvia became independent in the early 1920s Communists living in Latvia became immediately suspect. They were rounded up and imprisoned by the new government. Because of my father's leftist inclination as a student, he was also arrested and sent to a prison in Riga. He was tried and condemned to death. My grandfather was deeply distressed and sent a message to my father's eldest sister, who was married by then and living in Warsaw, to visit him before his execution.

Early Life in Dvinsk (Daugavpils)

She rushed to Riga and was walking from the railway station when by chance she met a Latvian officer of high rank whom she had known from earlier and happier times. He was surprised to meet her, and after a warm embrace asked the reason for her being there. She knew that he was an influential person and told him of the trouble that had befallen my father. Before parting from him she removed a valuable ring from her finger, gave it to him as a gift for his wife and asked him if he could help my father.

The day of my father's execution arrived. His cell door was opened; he was beaten up and allowed to go free without any explanation – obviously the Latvian officer had not forgotten the meeting with my aunt. On his way out he was called to the prison office, warned not to attend any political meetings and to change his political beliefs.

From this time my father became very religious for, during his imprisonment, he had spent long desperate hours praying and was convinced that his prayers had been answered. After a period of recuperation he went into his father's business, thus finally abandoning his engineering career. After my grandfather's death, and until the Russian invasion of Latvia in 1940, my father and his brother ran the business that, by then, dealt mainly in crockery.

Although my father was the younger of the two sons, he carried the burden of the business by virtue of his education. He travelled a great deal to Germany and Czechoslovakia, making valuable contact with suppliers including the renowned Rosenthal porcelain factory. As a result, my mother had beautiful monogrammed dinner and tea services and exquisite Czechoslovakian crystal. The Rosenthal factory gave me dolls and a miniature dinner set which was a replica of my mother's. The only remaining memento I own of those days is a small gilt china Kusnetzov miniature samovar my father gave to one of my uncles, who visited us from South Africa in 1932. This he subsequently passed on to me many years later.

My mother, one of nine children, lost her mother when still in her teens. Her father was one of the first pupils at the Vilna Teacher's Institute. They were not wealthy and he was only able to study for two years. He decided to follow the more lucrative trade of watchmaker, and became so interested in his new calling that he went to London to specialize in the making of chronometers.

He had married young, and took his bride with him to London. However, the London climate did not agree with her and they returned to Ponevej, Lithuania, where he opened a watch-making and jewellery shop. Due to the quality of his work, this became a highly successful venture. In later years, he became known for his great knowledge of Talmud (the Rabbinic commentary on the Old Testament) and was received with respect wherever he went.

He had nine children of whom four completed their university studies. Of these, my Uncle Avram read law in Heidelberg, Germany, and later became a celebrated lawyer. He knew eight languages, and I was told that to hear him in court was a privilege. People would close their shops to be present when they heard that he was appearing in a case and afterwards he would be carried shoulder-high from the courthouse.

Dina, the youngest of my mother's sisters, was considered a beauty and studied dentistry in Kiev. After completing her course in 1918, she contracted influenza when she was returning home by train and died soon afterwards. However, during this train journey she struck up a friendship with a woman by the name of Fania. Many years later when I came to South Africa and met my future husband's family, I was introduced to a lively, elderly lady referred to as Aunt Fanny Goldman. She immediately began questioning me about my background, and it transpired that she was the same Fania who had travelled with my Aunt Dina so many years before. She described the beautiful blonde plaits that crowned Dina's head as though the meeting 30 years previously was but yesterday. So many significant coincidences have occurred throughout my life that I refer to them mentally as 'truth stranger than fiction'.

My mother, Rebecca, studied music at the Berlin Conservatory. In 1927 she married my father and even this event carries an element of strangeness. My mother came to Dvinsk from Ponevej, her hometown, to attend the wedding of her best friend. At the wedding a young man approached her and made her acquaintance. Before her departure for

Early Life in Dvinsk (Daugavpils)

home she was invited by the same young man to accompany him on a walk. On the way a youngster rushed out from one of the gates, stood for a moment looking at my mother and announced: 'Here comes the bride and groom'. A year later the 'prophecy' came true and they were married. Two years later I arrived.

From 1936 until the German occupation of Latvia in 1941, we shared a double-storey brick house consisting of two flats, with my father's brother Isac, his wife Annia, his son Hertzel and also his daughter Masha who had been living in the ground floor section for some years before we moved in. Before that, we had lived in another part of town opposite my nursery school and later, my primary school.

Our new neighbours were Dr Silin and Dr Rosenblum. Dr Silin's daughter, Chava, and Dr Rosenblum's son, Lushia, were my constant companions in our backyard games. How well we remembered these times during the horrors we were to share only a few years later.

The yard was a miserable cobble-stoned place that never saw the sun because it was surrounded on three sides by tall buildings. One side of the yard consisted of a whole row of storerooms in which chickens and wood for winter were kept. However, the yard was not without its special attractions, amongst them the *dvornik* (the yardman) and his wife. They lived in a cellar, the portion of the building customarily reserved for *dvornik* families. The cellar was one large room with a cosy log fire in winter and, when one passed a *dvornik's* room, there was the inevitable smell of potatoes fried in sunflower seed oil. This was the cheapest form of food and the customary staple diet of the peasants. Most *dvorniks'* rooms would have a bed or two, depending on the size of the family, covered with a crocheted bedspread. Above the head of the bed hung an icon with a few dried leaves and flowers beneath it. A big, home-made pinewood table stood in the middle of the room with a vase holding paper or waxed flowers on a colourful embroidered tablecloth; this was surrounded by primitive wooden benches. The focal point of the room would be another icon hung on the wall or standing on a small shelf, in front of which a little red light flickered. On either side of the door was a small window, on the sills of which stood flowerpots containing geraniums, aspidistra or some cacti. The inevitable yard broom for summer sweeping, and a big spade for shovelling snow in winter, were kept on a rack by the door.

The *dvorniks* kept the buildings clean, swept the streets and the yard, and chopped wood for the tenants. They could be seen at the crack of dawn in winter dressed in their hats and sheepskin coats tied at the waist with a piece of rope or thong, clearing away the snow which had fallen during the night. Generally speaking, their job was not a pleasant one.

One day our *dvornik*'s wife gave birth to a baby and thus enriched our existence. For hours we would watch the baby being fed at the breast or being wrapped or unwrapped in yards and yards of cloth. These cloth strips were supposed to make the baby grow with straight legs but made her look like a mummy. She also wore a little crocheted bonnet and usually lay motionless. The climax of the whole episode came when the *dvornik*'s wife started feeding her baby on solids. She used to chew the food in her mouth and then feed the baby with it, whilst we stood there fascinated.

Another vivid memory was the market in Dvinsk. Fridays gave it a special atmosphere. The marketplace would be filled with peasants assembling from all the nearby villages. They would bring their wares to the market and after selling these, would go into town to do their shopping. I used to love going to market with mother and Nanny. What fun it was to go from cart to cart on which peasants sat displaying their wares. What an art it was to get the best value for your money; how many clay pots with sour cream had to be opened for my mother to be able to taste. She would pull a piece of straw from the cart, fold it in half, dip it into the cream and pop it into her mouth and, with eyes closed, would pronounce the verdict – good or otherwise. With tears in my eyes I would beg my mother to buy me a baby lamb or calf that stood, tied up to the cart. Eggs were scrutinized one by one against the light, before final completion of the deal. Of special interest was the fish market. There, predominantly Jewish fishwives, true to form, would try to attract attention. For the purchase of the fish, a technique all of its own was required. My mother, like all the others, would lift the gills of every fish until the desired shade of pink was found. Thereafter the weighing and bargaining would begin, as though it were a standard procedure.

My best friend was a girl who lived round the corner from us and attended the same nursery school. Her name was Chaya Treger. She was the tallest girl in our class and had the longest plaits in the school. She was always neat and spotless. However, those plaits were a great source of aggravation to her, for the boys could not resist pulling them. At singing lessons she always excelled herself. She spent a great deal of time in our home. We took our afternoon naps together, attended ballet school and went for walks with my Nanny. She lived in a single-storey house, reached by crossing a spacious yard that was entered through a wooden gate. On one side of the yard was a sandpit where we made mud-pies, and the other side was occupied by various tenants. Chaya's mother was a white-haired lady with a peaches and cream complexion. A grey cat whose basket stood near the kitchen door was an integral member of the family. The house had a small shady garden where we played most of the time. When her mother and a very smart aunt who lived with them were out, we would dress up in their shoes and dresses and parade for hours on end around the dining table and in the garden in a make-believe world of our own.

It was in 1936 when my parents decided to build our own flat. My friends and I used to love crossing the town to watch the builders at work. If we went at lunchtime, the aroma of charcoal-baked herring engulfed the whole place. What a treat it was for us to be invited to partake of the workers' meal! Eventually our beautiful new home was completed and we moved in.

My mother, who travelled frequently to Germany and Czechoslovakia, always brought back new ideas in furnishing so that every few months a change of décor would take place. I remember my parent's old oak bedroom suite, ornately carved, which I considered very beautiful. In its place a dark green matt-finished suite was installed. I could not see the improvement, for to my youthful eyes the straight plain lines and the very low bed had no appeal at all. It was nothing like the beautifully embellished beds I saw in fairy-tale illustrations. When, however, the same fate befell our dining room suite and the low straight sideboard replaced the tall one, I immediately took a great fancy to it. I especially liked the round table and the low sideboard in which it was easy to reach the drawers. I was even allocated a shelf for my dolls' crockery that I always made a point of showing off to interested, as well as to the not-so-interested, guests.

However, I had great misgivings about the curtains. They were extraordinary. Nothing like the beautiful rich red, green velvet or brocade drapes possessed by most of my friend's parents. To my unsophisticated eye, an ecru-coloured plain fishnet, stretched tightly on a brown shiny wooden frame, which surrounded each one of the four large windows, was not impressive, in spite of the great admiration of mother's friends. The fact that the fishnet was appliquéd with hand-crocheted bunches of grapes and leaves of the same ecru colour, was of no consequence. The wallpaper in that room was a lovely yellow which gave the room a sunny look all the year round. Even on bitterly cold winter days it seemed cosy and warm. A Persian carpet, so big that it needed four men to take it outside for cleaning, covered the floor. One of these was a mentally retarded man with a runny nose, who answered all questions with 'yes' or 'no'. In winter, my mother would engage him to carry wood for the oven up from the yard, and do all the odd jobs.

My room was heaven to me. I shared it with my beloved devoutly Catholic Nanny. There, during the days, I did my homework, played with my dolls and entertained my friends. At night Nanny would sit by my bed and tell me stories of the First World War, or read from my fairy-tale books that held me spellbound for hours. She taught me moral standards; 'Christian doctrine' – as she called it. On the quiet she taught me to say a prayer and cross myself, and always added: 'It will do your Jewishness no harm!' G–d was her shining light and she believed in Him implicitly. She admired my father for his deep belief in G–d and respected all the Jewish customs. The two of them would often set out in the early mornings together to attend their respective houses of worship.

She taught me to sew and knit; in fact, I often think that if there is anything at all good in me, it is partly due to her influence. She was my constant companion. Many times

Early Life in Dvinsk (Daugavpils)

during a thunderstorm that petrified me, my mother would find her sleeping on the floor next to my bed. Her love for me was boundless. My mother and she were great friends. She came to us when I was two and remained with us until the War. As my mother was constantly travelling, I looked upon her as my second mother.

For general education my parents engaged a German fräulein whom I disliked intensely. It was rather strange that I remember so little about her apart from the fact that she spoke very bad Russian. This disability of hers was my only source of amusement in our daily encounters. For some reason, perhaps due to my ignorance, I did not associate her with Germany at all, until later horrors connected with Germans created a false link. I remember that my first glimpse of her was in the room called the 'salon'. The room, which looked forbidding to me and my friends and which we were officially allowed only to peep into, was the main entertaining space of our house. Two divans were arranged in an 'L' shape, with cerise-coloured covers which hung down to the floor at each end contrasting strongly with the pale yellow walls. A lamp with matching lampshade and long fringes stood at the junction of the divans.

I was allowed into the salon to practice on the piano and have lessons from a renowned teacher, Wolper-Rabinovitch. To me, and to my friends whom she also taught, she was known as the *vedma* (the witch). She was short, wore thick glasses and had a violent temper. She never accepted any excuse from me for not having prepared my lesson. I still have a vivid recollection of her getting so agitated with my playing that she broke two keys of the piano. My mother used to love this room and spent a great deal of time there, reading or playing the piano. Father would occasionally join her with his violin. Together they would make music, my father singing his favourite aria – 'Donna e mobile' – from *Rigoletto*. I am quite convinced he knew no other song for he never sang anything else.

I was very happy in our new home which was surrounded by a large garden. On three sides chestnut trees bordered the entire length of the high fence. English May was in abundance. Amongst all this greenery stood an old *besedka* (summer house). There, in days gone by, afternoon tea would be served from the samovar. Now the besedka was broken down and dilapidated and we were allowed to make full use of it. When not playing-in the garden we would be engaged in a game of croquet and, looking back, I think much of my childhood fun emerged from playing this game at home or in the *dacha*.* In winter, the garden would be knee-deep in snow. We threw snowballs and built huge snowmen with carrots for noses and charcoal for eyes. All these activities were watched by the ravens, which sat on the snow-laden trees and croaked their support. Soon after the snow melted, blue irises made their appearance along the garden path. An enormous pear tree, perhaps a hundred years old, stood on one side of the garden within sight of my parents' bedroom window. In spring this tree, together with apple and cherry trees in blossom, was a sight never to be forgotten. Many varieties of berries grew along the picket fence that separated the garden from the yard. In early spring the yard would be full of baby chickens bought at the market, which would become full-grown birds by the Jewish New Year in autumn. For my cousin Marsha and me it was a sad time because the chickens that had become our pets had to be slaughtered. Many a tear was shed in trying to spare one or other of them.

The annual rhythm of Jewish festivals gladdened my existence. The eve of Yom Kippur was a solemn time in our home. My father, being very religious, took pride in adhering to all the Jewish customs. Succoth was a particularly happy time. Father was solely responsible for the building of the *succah* (traditional festive eating booth), which was a major undertaking; but my duty lay in providing the decorations – a task I enjoyed tremendously.

There was great commotion before the Pesach (Passover) festivities. In early spring, my Nanny and I took numerous trips to dip the cooking utensils in a drum of boiling water at some place or other, to make them kosher. The changing of crockery was exciting. For the first time in that season the double windows were opened wide and cleaned. The paper

---

*Dacha: a summerhouse usually built at the seaside, lake or forest and not far from the city where one lived. Usually all three summer months were spent there.

Early Life in Dvinsk (Daugavpils)

strips that sealed the gaps to keep out the cold during winter were removed. The carpet was taken up and the floor was polished while the aroma of polish permeated the entire house. It was a smell I always associated with the arrival of guests or a high holiday. The *matzos* would be delivered in big brown packets in such quantities that I thought there would be enough for the entire year.

At last, the *seder* – a communal dinner held on the eve of Pesach to which friends are invited – arrived. On this occasion, the *Haggadah*, the story of the exodus of the Jews from Egypt, is read. Outside Israel two such dinners are held on two consecutive nights. On our return from synagogue the table would glitter with cut glass and candles. The guests would be placed and my father would sit in a chair propped up on pillows, a look of achievement on his friendly, open face. He conducted the *seder* and read the *Haggadah* with joy and merriment. Course after course would be served. Soup with the *Kneidlach* (*matzo* balls) would arrive last instead of early in the meal, due to a strange Eastern European custom. While this was served, the children would think of some mischief to come up with. How could I possibly forget the paper tail which we pinned on to the back of one of my parents' annual guests – a funny-looking bachelor who was supposed to have an excellent knowledge of the Talmud, but could not make ends meet. The climax of the evening would come with the finding of the *afikomen** and its sale to my father.

With the approach of May a new and exciting chapter dawned – the end of the school year. Although I enjoyed school and was an average pupil holidays were always something to look forward to. My position in class was in the first ten, although my aspirations were higher. Mathematics and drawing were my worst subjects, but my mother was good at art and my father was good at figures, and with the willing help with my homework, I managed to hold my position in class. I did well in handicrafts, due to my Nanny's influence, and usually got a good mark for gym. The credit for that goes to the ballet school run by Madam Mirtzeva. I loved

---

*Afikomen: A piece of *matzo* that the head of the family hides. The children find it, but do not return it to the father until he has paid a forfeit.

ballet and worshipped our prima ballerina, Galina Manshevskaya. Great excitement enveloped our studio before the annual concert that took place at the Railway Theatre. What sweet memories of the daily rehearsals, trying on costumes, sleepless nights before the performance and, finally, appearing on stage to face the hushed audience! For this alone, life was worth living. The 'ah's' and 'oh's' if your name happened to be mentioned in print filled me with pride. The love of ballet has never left me.

One aspect of my education that I did not enjoy was English lessons. These were given to me by a stout, dark and greasy-looking man. He was well travelled and very intelligent, but I appreciated neither quality. The only thing he successfully taught me was to recite Oscar Wilde's *The Happy Prince* by heart, and at the slightest provocation I would do so.

My birthday on 1 May meant that our departure for our holiday at the dacha was approaching. My wardrobe required attention, and for this and other minor sewing alterations a woman named Hena was called in. She was a little old spinster who waddled rather than walked. When her hands were not occupied at the sewing machine, they were always tucked under her bosom as if she were afraid of losing it. She worked in my room, and every few minutes would summon me to try on this or that dress. For my party dresses I used to be taken to ORT – a Jewish organization that provided technical training in all fields to the underprivileged – where the sewing department had a fine reputation. The girls took great pride in executing their orders to the very best of their ability. A young girl whose face I do not recollect, although I vividly remember the crown of her frizzy head of hair, fussed around me for what seemed like hours on end whilst I stood on a little stool, bored stiff.

My mother's support for this organization, which has done so much to establish skill-training programmes for the underprivileged throughout the world, goes back to her days of study in Berlin beginning in 1922. As a young girl her talent for music led her to studying the piano. As she progressed it was decided that she should travel to Berlin to continue her studies at the conservatory of music. Travelling alone on the train she struck up a conversation with two men in the

Early Life in Dvinsk (Daugavpils)

compartment. One of these was particularly friendly; his name was Sigalnitsky. Because of her obvious nervousness at having to find her way as a stranger in a foreign city once she arrived in Berlin, he offered to introduce her to his wife and family who, he assured her, would be happy to assist. On their arrival in Berlin, they were met by Sigalnitsky's wife Elna and son Israel. This was the start of a long warm friendship. Sigalnitsky was an engineer by profession and one of the founders of ORT.

To set my mother up so that she could get on with her studies, her new friends arranged for her to lodge with close friends of theirs – these were an old father and two spinster daughters. They became very fond of my mother and introduced her to other friends who were part of the 'intelligensia' of Berlin at that time. She was introduced to many famous musicians and artists and her taste in the arts and things intellectual were much influenced by the challenging society of which she was now part. Until her old age she loved telling the story of the time she was invited to an ORT anniversary party and was introduced to the already great Albert Einstein and his secretary, next to whom she was placed at the tea table. Even her taste for contemporary furniture could be explained by her contact with artists of the famous Bauhaus School.

My mother's dressmaker was the owner of a salon and was known for her beautiful clothes. She was responsible for the design of my school uniform, which consisted of a black alpaca apron over a navy blue dress with white collar and cuffs. Stockings and black lace-up shoes competed the ensemble.

My birthdays, like the ballet soirées, were the highlights of my life and were always celebrated with great pomp and ceremony. My mother's contribution to this occasion was a table laden to breaking point with the most beautifully decorated cakes and cookies. It took both her and my Nanny weeks to prepare everything. In winter the children, as if conforming to special rules, would be dressed in white stockings, patent leather or white shoes and their best party dresses. In summer the long stockings were replaced by short white socks. All would arrive holding their presents, of which they were immediately relieved by the birthday girl. A special treat at summer parties was ice-cream. Whilst the party was in progress, my father would labour in the kitchen turning the handle of the ice-cream machine, praying that the proportions of sugar, cream and milk were right. The danger of the mixture not setting was always present. With great triumph he would come out of the kitchen with the bucket of ice-cream, place it in the middle of the garden, and invite everyone to cool off. The stampede then began.

The programme for the parties varied little. Games – such as 'the broken telephone' or 'musical chairs' – were a must. After tea, the cultural part of the party would take place. A girl or boy, standing on a chair, would start reciting a poem that would be forgotten halfway through, or some prodigy would play, badly, 'Für Elise' or the 'Blue Danube' waltz on the piano. Winter birthday parties had an added attraction. At a given moment the lights were switched off and sparklers were lit. The belle of the ball would stand in the middle of the ring while the birthday song was sung.

The summer months from May to August were spent at our *dacha* in the popular holiday resort on Lake Stropi. There on the shore of this beautiful sheet of water, days were halcyon and completely divorced from our organized life in Dvinsk. After the packing was done, the furniture was covered with sheets and Anton with his horse and cart would arrive. He would be greeted by all the members of the family as if he were a long-lost friend. For him this was a standing engagement from one year to the next. The luggage was piled high on the cart. Nanny with my little dog in her arms would accompany Anton while Mother and I would follow by bus, travelling past peaceful summer fields. Father would remain in Dvinsk during the week and on Friday evenings would come to spend the weekends with us. The time spent at the dacha was very relaxed. In the mornings we used to go to the lake for a swim, go for boat rides or play volleyball. Along the edge of the lake – about 30 feet or so from the shore – stood colourful changing booths reached by rickety little wooden bridges to which boats were moored. At lunch time the crowd would disperse, and after lunch silence descended on Stropi. Siestas were strictly observed. Some took their rest in hammocks – weather permitting – and others on the grass or in *chaise-longes*. Occasionally the lazy summer afternoon would be interrupted by the melodious voice of a peasant woman chanting her wares. She would come from across the lake, a yoke on her shoulders, bearing baskets of fresh berries or the season's first fruits. Sometimes others would offer fresh milk or cream. At teatime, or 'five-o'clock', we would leave for the teagarden. While the adults talked and had their tea, the children would pay on the swings or lick their ice-creams, which were served between two round wafers. Often we would go for walks and would return with armfuls of beautiful peonies that grew in profusion, permeating the whole area with their magnificent scent.

On special occasions we would go into the forest. We picked berries or mushrooms or just walked deep into the forest to climb the Scarbovka, the local mountain. From early childhood we knew where the wild berries grew, where to find the best blackberries, which mushrooms were edible and what to avoid. With the approach of evening, the children were put to bed and Stropi took on a different character. Parties, music and card games kept the grownups busy.

On Friday mornings, at about eleven o'clock, the servants would wait at the bus stops along the main road for the big baskets laden to the brim with provisions for the weekend, which would be lowered from the bus to the waiting servants. Ours, like the others, would be dispatched from Dvinsk after the Friday morning market.

Occasionally my aunt, Berta Dukarevitz, who lived in Poland, would come to spend the summer holidays with us. One year she arrived with her two-year-old daughter, Basia, a spoilt little thing but extremely clever for her age. When not fighting with me over a beautiful ball that I had been given on my last birthday, now my prized possession, I enjoyed her company very much. My aunt's second daughter, Franka, who was 18 years older than Basia, always remained at home. She was educated by a French governess and was entrusted to my mother's care as a travelling companion during my mother's frequent long trips. Franka had beautiful titian-coloured hair and married very early. Her husband was the son of a wealthy family by the name of Chwat who lived in

Lodz. He was an engineer and an officer in the Polish Army. There was much excitement before my parents left for her wedding, and I clearly recollect the beautiful black dress with its blue sailor collar and silver embroidery that my mother made for the occasion. The Chwat's married bliss was short lived, however, as war followed a few years later and her husband was killed in action.

In 1938, to my surprise and delight, the Treger family were our neighbours on holiday in Stropi. That last summer of peace stands out very vividly in my memory. Chaya and I spent a lot of time together making clay pots and swimming. At the end of the holiday I said goodbye to that family, for they were going to join their father in Africa. Most people considered Africa to be the other side of the world as few people had any contact with it, but to me it was not quite so remote because of the two uncles I had living there. I knew from photographs that it was very hot; and that they were always dressed in white trousers and shirtsleeves and wore panama hats. In most of the photographs they were either standing next to a car or sitting in it waving their hats. It is only now I realize that the reason for this was that to own a car was a symbol of impressive achievement and they were very proud of their vehicles. Dr Doolittle, Hugh Lofting's great character, also contributed to my knowledge of Africa.

At the end of summer when we returned home from the dacha, the garden would be full of marigolds and other yellow flowers – a beautiful sight to welcome us home. To this day, the scent of marigolds filling the air triggers off my memory as I walk in my garden in Johannesburg, pick an iris, or – in late summer – a marigold, and find myself in a dream of bittersweet memories of my childhood back in Dvinsk in the years before the Second World War.

The Second World War

I became aware of Germany, and Hitler in particular, one afternoon after school. My cousin Masha and I on certain afternoons during the week would go to the shops of our respective fathers. We were usually given ten centimes each to spend on our favourite tidbits – a Danish pastry from Kissins on Vladimir Street or a string of dry bagels from the Mitrofanovs to be worn around one's neck, or the very special toffee from Francis' which justified a walk through the park to the other side of town. On this particular afternoon, instead of the usual friendly greeting and a kiss from my father, I was told to wait and keep quiet. My father, mother and uncle, with horror on their faces, were speaking to some strangers in German. The spokesman for the group, with tears in his eyes and choking with emotion, was telling my parents of events in Germany and of the terrors the Jews had experienced since Hitler's coming to power. The horrors of the *Kristallnacht* (the Night of the Broken Glass), the beating up of Jews at random and seizure of Jewish property, shops and businesses, the destruction of synagogues and Jewish books were all part of their story. Although they were now penniless and had nowhere to go, they were lucky to have escaped with their lives. 'Was there anything my father could do to assist them?' was their question.

The flood of refugees increased day by day. The whole town was agog with the revelations of those unfortunate people. How could a thing like this happen? How could the world allow it? Innocent people deprived of their homes, their country – Germany – the country many Jews had given their lives for in the First World War not so long ago. Civilized Germany – their motherland; the Germany they loved, the Germany they had made major contributions to in economic development and cultural life – had now viciously rejected them. They were reduced to become fleeing refugees. Professor, lawyer and tramp – all were herded together and evicted. Some of the refugees became my parents' guests and Dr Belinson, a friend of the family, married one of them.

In 1939, Germany invaded Poland. The ripples from events in Germany were now beginning to engulf us. Letters from my aunt in Poland became more distressing. The mood in our home grew somber. The last letter my parents received from Poland informed them that the Jews were now in ghettos and were starving. In a roundabout manner they wrote 'birds are being shot', making my parents understand that it was Jews who were being shot. This last event involved me personally, because a large parcel of food and clothing was made up and nanny and I pulled it on my sledge to the post office.

Whilst the upheavals in Poland continued, an event of a slightly different nature affected us and the other Baltic States. We were on the threshold of experiences, which although not quite as traumatic as the ones in Germany and Poland, were about to bring great changes into our lives. I was 11 years old on Latvia's Independence Day, an event always celebrated with great enthusiasm and ceremony, culminating in grand parades throughout the country. This year, Dvinsk was honoured by a visit from our Prime Minister, Ulmanis. The town eagerly anticipated his arrival. As usual, children and grownups alike would go to my cousin Abrasha's home to watch the parade from their balcony. Their building was situated on Riga Street, not far from the station, which on this day was the focal point as the Prime Minister was to lead the parade from there and along Riga Street into town. We stood on the balcony and waited the whole afternoon, but the Prime Minister did not arrive. We were all very puzzled and disappointed until my parents switched on the radio at home and heard the Prime Minister announce in a trembling voice that the parade had had to be cancelled. With German consent, the Russians had crossed the Latvian border. He asked that we should remain calm. Within a few hours, being near the border, the Russian Army was marching through Dvinsk. From then on, events moved with lightning speed. How little did we suspect the tragic extent to which Dvinsk, Russia, and the Jews in particular, would be affected by the ravages of war in the years immediately ahead. My parents, having had experience of the First World War, anticipated shortages of food and clothing, and laid-in stocks. Big bags of sugar and flour and tins of various kinds and sizes were delivered and packed in cupboards. For the first time in my life, a ready-made coat three sizes too big was bought for me. I was taken to an *angros* (wholesaler) where shoes of various sizes and types were bought. It was the 'tango' (tangerine colour) ones that particularly took my fancy. Although two sizes too large, I was allowed to wear them for a while as everything had to appear worn to disguise its newness. We children were not aware of the political implications or economic changes that were taking place. We enjoyed the processions of workers, the red banners and the singing of the 'International', rejoicing in the denouncing of the capitalist regime. Posters and slogans about Lenin and Stalin were put up on walls. I was wearing my red blouse as a sign of welcome to the Russians. It was summer. We had time to observe and even to participate in some events, without understanding their significance, whilst we enjoyed our school holidays.

At home, my parents and their friends often discussed the changes that were occurring and I could feel their anxiety. With the arrival of the army, instructions were issued to us to open our homes to the soldiers. Irrespective of the size of the house, each family was only allowed a fixed area per person. All the buildings above a certain size were nationalized. Our building was divided into two flats, and my parents were lucky to retain ownership. However, this did not preclude us from having to make room for a Russian officer.

He was a high-ranking Tartar, very well built and extremely charming. His Russian was appalling, which I found paradoxical in view of his high rank. He would often go to sleep fully clothed without even taking off his boots, and he never wore socks. He liked to do his own cooking on a primus stove in the kitchen. He would supply us with a whole salmon and was generous with vodka. Not long after his arrival, he informed us that his wife and children would be joining him. His wife, it appeared, was an expert in the art of preparing pilaff. In great detail and for hours on end, he would tell my mother about the ingredients required for this exotic dish and how it was customary to serve and eat it, mostly with the hands, from a common dish. It sounded exciting and I was counting the days to her arrival. His wife duly arrived with two little children who could not speak a word of Russian. This, however, did not prevent my cousin and me, or the children from the whole neighbourhood, from playing with them. To all of us they were a great novelty.

On reflection, I realize how wise it was of my parents to lay in stocks, because soon after the arrival of the wives of the Russian officers, the shops were empty. They came from all parts of Russia, where shortages had prevailed since the Revolution. Latvia, and the Baltic States generally, were a paradise to them. They had never seen or known such luxury and bought everything they could lay their hands on. They would wear a nightdress to go dancing out of sheer ignorance. Within a month all the businesses, including my father's, were nationalized. The owners simply handed over the keys to the authorities without any hope of compensation. Most of the factory owners and other businessmen were out of work and were not given employment. They were labelled capitalists and exploiters and as such were enemies of the people. Only in very rare cases, if there were no one available from the proletariat class, would they be given employment in a responsible position.

My father, now that his business had been nationalized, was afraid of the consequences of unemployment. He decided to take advantage of his earlier sufferings in prison in the name of Communism. He found all the evidence of his convictions, submitted it to the right authorities and, shortly afterwards, to our surprise and his delight, became a hero. He was given an important job as an engineer on the railways, a profession he had not pursued since his university days. Even my Uncle Isac, his brother, was given some privileges.

September was the beginning of a new school year. It became evident that my old Hebrew school would not reopen. Religion was outlawed, and my parents had to decide to which school to send me. A Jewish school was considered, and I was even taken to our friend, Mrs Lena Rosenberg, a noted teacher; but she was no longer permitted to take private pupils. My parents were reluctant to send me to a local Russian or Latvian school, because there was much anti-Semitism amongst the predominantly non-Jewish children. Then a new Russian school for the children of the Russian Army officers was opened. A limited number of children of local 'Members of the Proletariat' were also admitted. With my father's new position, my cousin Masha and I were included. I was very happy in my new school. I adjusted quickly to the new environment and made many friends. I soon caught up with Russian literature and maintained my usual position in class. Although this school was run in two shifts because of the shortage of Russian teachers, I soon got used to going to school in the afternoon and returning home for supper instead of lunch.

Before leaving for school, I would knock on our kitchen floor three times with a broom to say I was ready, and my cousin would come out of her front door downstairs and wait for me. Together we would walk to school, which took about half an hour. In addition to the usual school subjects, a few new ones were introduced. Apart from the thorough study of the Russian Constitution, *Politruks* (political instructors) were brought in, and we spent considerable time on political instruction. They gave lectures on the evils of the West and the wonders of Communism. I now saw everything in the West in a new light. America consisted of capitalists and exploiters – both dirty words in the Russian lexicon – who were parasites living off the labours of the starving masses of the proletariat, whereas one could not help but admire and marvel at the quoted examples of equality and opportunity for all under the Communist regime. We children were completely taken up with the idea of Communism. How easy it is to indoctrinate children; how dangerous propaganda can be! It soon became my great ambition to join the Pioneers (a junior Communist league) and having finally achieved this, I was rewarded with a red tie. This was given only after taking the Pioneer oath with great solemnity. I was bursting with pride, but my parents were not impressed in the least by all of this. Although they made friends with the Russians and were superficially happy in their company, their lifestyle changed drastically. They stopped entertaining. I was given strict instructions not to divulge what was going on at home. No new dresses were made for me during that year. The only new article of clothing each member of our family received that winter was a pair of *valinki* (high felt boots), worn with galoshes when the snow started to melt.

Pesach of that year was celebrated very quietly. There were no visitors. The *Haggadah* was cut short. There was no gaiety or entertainment for us children. My parents were strained and tensed at every knock. On parting with friends, one often heard the words 'May it not be worse for us.' We lived from day to day not knowing what to expect. My parents were troubled by the uncertain future, and almost every day they would discuss the disappearance of some person they knew.

One morning, a phone-call awoke us with the most terrible news. Some of our relatives and many of our friends had been taken to the station to be deported to Siberia. All of them belonged to the capitalist class and were considered enemies of the people. They therefore had to be removed. Police had entered their homes, given them 15 minutes to get their belongings together and had taken them away. The deportation of the rich from the Baltic States was part of a general plan by the Russians to clear the area of 'political enemies of the people'. In effect, it turned out to be a blessing in disguise for many of the people, and for Jews in particular. The majority of them would hardly have survived the concentration camps yet to come. My parents, at the time, considered themselves lucky not to be included in the evacuation. However, in retrospect, if we had been given the choice, there would have been no doubt in our minds. Siberia would have been a paradise compared with what was to happen.

Almost to the year of the Russian occupation, on 22 June 1941, Dvinsk was shattered by the news that Germany had declared war on Russia and troops had already crossed the Latvian border.

I can never forget the moment when we children were playing pavement hopscotch and I noticed my mother coming from town. When she reached us perspiring and pale, she blurted out the terrible news that war had broken out. To me it seemed the end of the world was upon us. For the people of

Dvinsk it was the beginning of the dramatic road to victory – or so they thought. They had such faith in the might of the Red Army that no other fate could be foreseen. We did hear that in some other towns evacuation points were being organized but in our town there were none.

Within days the railway station was choked with people – mainly Lithuanian refugees – who had started to pour in as they fled the advancing Germans. Having filled the rows of platforms they spilled over into the streets and park outside, a bewildered mass of humanity not knowing where to find refuge. Children were looking for lost parents and panicking parents were screaming their children's names. The frightful screech of air raid sirens rent the nights that followed, anticipating the horrors to come. People were contacting police or military institutions for information or instructions. The gist of the response appeared to be, 'Run, if you can'. Many government officials were already putting their advice into practice and managed to flee. Those who could not find a place on the cattle trucks being marshaled in the goods yard filled prams or carts with their belongings, children and the elderly and started the forlorn march to the nearest Russian border. Bombing of the roads began and the tragedy of war started to unfold.

On my mother's instructions a routine for immediate survival was established. All empty utensils were filled with water in case the water supply was cut off. Loaves of bread were bought from which rusks were made. These and other precautions were introduced based on experience acquired from living through the First World War, which had begun almost exactly 25 years earlier. Action plans were debated by the adults. If the Russians retreated, the men would try to get to Russia. Perhaps we should all flee? Perhaps it would not be so bad? It might be wise to wait and see. We decided to wait and see.

That very afternoon the sirens sounded and German planes flew into Latvia and over Dvinsk. The battle was on. All of us, except my father, rushed to the cellar. The cellar had always been used for storing barrels of sauerkraut, pickled cucumbers, jars of fat, and other provisions that needed to be kept cool in the hot summer weather. It was beneath the kitchen stairs and gave us children a sense of security. My father refused to go down into the cellar, maintaining that whatever happened would be the will of G–d. I wonder if he had some sort of premonition that life would soon be over for him? The rest of us spent most of the following week in the cellar whilst the sirens sounded and bombs were exploding all the time. The adults would go up into the house to prepare food, wash and change and listen to the daily news bulletin on the radio. During the rare periods of silence, the children could go into the garden to watch the sky, only to rush back underground at the approach of a new wave of planes. We used to take bets on which plane belonged to which side and how many would be shot down. The German planes had a distinct high-pitched whine. Every now and then someone would rush in to report on which houses had received direct hits and how many casualties there had been during the day. The corner of our house was hit, ripping away the side of the dining room, but not even that made my father change his mind about joining us in the cellar.

Time dragged on. Nobody knew what was happening. The situation was confusing as conflicting claims were made by both sides. On the fourth day we heard that incendiary bombs had been dropped on the city. It became evident that the Russians were retreating. We were all panic-stricken. Father decided to make a dash for the last convoy composed of retreating Russians and refugees. Unfortunately the refugees were all turned back at the border. Within a day my father was back. More incendiary bombs were dropped. The city was burning. Time was running out for us.

Suddenly my father rushed into the cellar to tell us to get out. The houses nearby were on fire. We ran up the stairs and everyone grabbed whatever they could. Jersey upon jersey was put on me. Now I realized that the coat, which only a year ago had been three sizes too big for me, fitted. A bundle was pushed into my arms. I grabbed my little dog and we hurried out into the street. All around us houses blazed. We ran to the corner of the block and turned round to see our house engulfed in flames.

There was chaos everywhere. Frantic adults, lost children, mothers and fathers with babies in their arms and dogs were all trapped in this inferno. They were rushing in every direction, shouting 'There is no way to get through – try the next street, the next...'. Eventually, we could see no way out. We made a dash through a tunnel of fire formed by the burning buildings on either side of the street. The heat was unbearable. Patients from the nearby hospital were crawling on all fours in their nightclothes, crying, shouting, begging, to be helped. This particular scene haunts me to this day. We could not stop to help them. Our only thought was to survive long enough to reach the river where we hoped we would escape from the fire. On several occasions when we were on the point of collapse, we would try and rest for a few minutes on the steps of a building or shop, only to hear shouts – 'Fire...run!' – and again the street would be filled with people running like ants in all directions.

Eventually, we arrived at a building facing the river. We went into the lobby and sat on the stairs. Sweat was pouring from our faces as we sat there dry-mouthed and panting, too exhausted and shocked to speak.

It was June, the middle of summer, and in addition to the intense heat of the burning city, all of us were encased in layers and layers of jerseys and dresses. The question uppermost in our minds was – what next? We rested awhile; the fire did not spread, but every now and then a bomb would explode and there was the sound of gunfire. Then suddenly silence descended. My father decided to go out and see what was happening. The news was disheartening – much of the city had burned down. Charred corpses lay all over the streets. There was no sign of Russians or Germans. We decided to go and see if any of our friends' houses had escaped the conflagration. The walk through the still-smouldering city was ghastly.

Eventually, we reached a friend's home. The house was still standing, but they had been evacuated to Siberia so the neighbours took us into their already overcrowded home. My Nanny decided to go and find out whether her uncle had survived. He lived in a little wooden house that he had built himself in a suburb called Novoye Stronynie (the newly built part). This area was little affected by the fire, and she soon returned with the news that he was well and that she would stay with him. She took our little dog with her and left.

For several days corpses lay around the city. Of the neighbourhood we had known little more than blackened rubble remained. There was evidence everywhere that the Russians had put up a desperate resistance. After some days German soldiers began to make their appearance. Queues for bread were forming in some parts of town. The city was slowly awakening from its nightmare.

My parents went to our burnt-out house to try and salvage what they could. They dug out the silver and gold they had buried in the garden. Luckily, the gold coins they had cemented into the wall survived the fire and they were able to retrieve them. All this, besides the valuables we had given to my Nanny during the Russian occupation, was stored at her uncle's home.

The German Army arrived in full force and streets were crowded with soldiers. Field kitchens were set up at various points. One of them was across the road from where we were now living. The chef, a friendly middle-aged soldier, would often dish out leftovers to the children hanging around his kitchen. I soon got to know him, and every few days he would give me a big chunk of butter. Now and then an officer or a soldier would visit us. They were usually very courteous and would have a cup of tea or coffee and tell us about their families and their war experiences. Once an officer, who was drinking tea in the kitchen, told us that if the Germans continued at this rate with so little resistance from the Russians, they would be drinking tea in Moscow in a week's time! All this friendliness hardly prepared us for the drastic change in German attitude that was shortly to follow.

On Sunday, 29 July, *Obersturmführer* SS Günter Talbert, the German officer in charge of the city, issued an order instructing all Jewish men between the ages of 16 and 60 to report to the market place. Most of the men complied without suspicion or hesitation. They were rounded up with the help of the Latvian *Isargs* (members of the Fascist organization who were, as we later discovered, willing helpers in all the German activities concerning the destruction of the Jews). The men were divided into groups with a German or a Latvian overseer. Each group was taken to a different part of town to

The Second World War

clean up the city. On the first day the men were in good spirits, although the thought had crossed the minds of some that it was strange that only Jews had been singled out for the task.

Even stranger was the fact that after work the men were not allowed to return to their homes. This created suspicion in spite of the various reasons that were bandied about. Some Jews even thought that it was to save time and to eliminate the difficulties of rounding up the men each morning!

On several occasions, my mother, like all the other women, went to investigate the whereabouts of the menfolk. Mother would return from seeing father, bearing bits of bread, soap, or whatever he had salvaged from the cleaning operations. As the days passed, it became known that some of the wives could not find their husbands amongst the work parties. Rumours began to circulate that these men had been shot and the more the town was restored to order, the fewer were the remaining men. Many conflicting reports were heard. Some doubted the stories regarding the shooting and dismissed them as impossible. Why should they be shot? What crimes had they committed? They were probably being sent away to do other work out of town. But rumours of the shootings continued. One day my mother returned from town in a very agitated state. She could not find my father. The men she had found would not tell what had happened to the others. Rumours of shooting persisted. Someone who lived not far from the prison had heard shooting throughout the night. She went to the prison again and this time found my father there in a terrible state. His eyes were swollen and tears were running down his face. He told her of the horrifying night they had spent. Uncle Isac and many other men were called out, made to dig their own graves, and shot. He was sure that the same fate would befall him and the remaining men. Mother returned with this terrible news. Uncle Isac's wife and her daughter Martha, who had been living with us, fainted. We were all crying, mourning my uncle's death.

The next day when my mother went to see my father in prison, no one was there – the prison was empty. The men were gone. All enquiries were useless. As she was making her way home she encountered someone who told her that they had seen lorry-loads of men being transported from the prison the previous night. They had been taken in the direction of the outskirts of the town. She went there hoping to find father, but instead she encountered the most horrifying sight; horse-drawn carts full of men's clothing were passing her, the ghastly truth dawned on her – he was no more... She staggered into the house; there was no need to ask what had happened. 'They are all gone', she whispered, 'murdered in cold blood!'

It was only years after the War that the reality of the prison horror and the extent of the cruelty experienced by the men immediately before their murder became known. The actual story was the stuff of nightmares.

The Germans and their local Latvian police assistants under the command of the inhuman Günter Talbert were instructed to search all houses and lofts for Jews who may not have complied with the orders issued on 29 July. All those who had complied, and the later prisoners who were taken by force to the market place, were made to stand for hours in columns of five. Two people were shot dead. Their names were Leizer Goldberg and Myer Myerowitch. Their crime, wanting to say goodbye to their wives, who stood terrified on the side of the square. Towards evening the mass of men were directed to move in the direction of the prison. Where there was resistance the columns were forced along with the willing help of the Latvian *Isargs*.

While the column was marching along the embankment, the Jews were ordered to sing 'Katusha', a Russian song. The people would not sing. The police started attacking Ishik Rudashevsky, one of those who were silent, until he bled. Again the order to sing came and the Jews started to sing very softly. The column approached the embankment of the Dvina River. Further along on the road they turned right and realized that they were heading for the prison.

The gates were closed, but a well-turned out German soldier started shouting at the top of his voice that they were all guilty of all the sins of the world, and that they would all be shot now. 'I will give you three minutes to pray, and ask forgiveness for your sins,' he shouted.

Suddenly he started shooting into the crowd and wounded many of the people. The women who had escorted the column started crying, but the soldiers shouted at them to be quiet. A shout from another SS officer followed: 'If ten Jews can be found among you, who are prepared to die for the others, I will let the rest go free.' From all sides hands were lifted. One volunteer was the Chief Rabbi Alter Fuks, who had replaced the world-renowned Rabbi Rogachevsky. The people who had volunteered were made to face the brick wall. The rifles were cocked, but the order to shoot did not come. The officer was having cruel fun.

A more interesting spectacle was devised. Before allowing the people into the yard of the prison, long benches were placed across the entrance and the people – in particular the elderly ones – were told to jump over the benches, in a certain number of seconds. The SS were counting the seconds on their watches, and shooting.

After the survivors were allowed into the prison, they spent a bitter night as best they could. In the morning they were all chased out into the yard. The younger, and stronger, Jews were taken to work in town, while the older ones were sent into the cellars and locked up. Every day groups of these men were taken out and shot in the railway park across from the prison in a macabre routine. The groups that were to be shot in the morning were made to stand, shoulder to shoulder, all night. At four in the morning the Head of Police would walk around with a stick, and motion the condemned in the cellars to stand five in a row. They were then marched across the embankment, to the park. After they had dug their own graves, they were made to undress, were shot, and then thrown into the graves. The dead and the not-so-dead were all covered with soil. This was done by those who remained – until all had perished.

When chimney sweep Iosif Zorum would not obey, they beat him up. Still he refused and, grabbing an iron bar, he brought it down on the head of one of the overseers, splitting it open. He also wounded a few others. He was shot immediately.

On 15 July from 11.00 p.m. that night until 11.00 a.m. the next day, one of the largest murder *Aktions** took place. In a secret document, of 16 July, it is revealed that Jewish men

---

*Aktion: the violent rounding-up of Jews who were gathered from surrounding buildings and then sorted for the death process. This selection process was implemented in most ghettos and camps throughout Europe.

brought to prison were immediately shot and buried in previously prepared graves. The operational commander in Daugavpils succeeded in having 1,150 men killed in just 12 hours.

We were not given much time to mourn our dear ones, because it was time for stage two to begin. With the aid of the local population, a finger was pointed at every Jew. There was no escaping. This made the task of the German SS, who were rounding up the Jews, very easy. Much of the population who had lost their homes and possessions during the fire, were only too happy to have the opportunity of ridding the city of the Jews and occupying their vacant homes with official blessing. What a windfall for them!

The Ghetto

Having got rid of the men, the next stage began. Jews were being caught on the streets and in the squares. At this stage my mother and I, together with my cousin Mascha and her mother, were staying in a flat belonging to some friends. One day there was a loud knock on the door. A Latvian and an SS soldier came in shouting *'Raus! Raus! Schnell!'* (Out! Out! Quickly!) – and began searching the flat.

Mother had the presence of mind to grab me by the hand and we ran into the street and to our distant relative, Dr Magid. He was a dentist, and allowed us to live for the time being in his own home as he attended to the dental needs of the Germans. We stayed with them awhile, until his wife and daughter were sent with us to the ghetto. He remained in town to continue his work. In the meantime, Mascha, her mother and our friends, the Gradeises who lived round the corner, were all taken to the synagogue. Cilia Gradeis, the younger daughter, recalled the events many years later. They were kept there for several days without food, water or adequate sanitary facilities. There was no place to lie down. She and her sister, however, could speak perfect Latvian as both had attended a Latvian school. Realizing what was in store for them, they persuaded the Latvian on guard at the synagogue to allow them to go out for a while. They fled to Cilia's violin teacher, Paul Kruminsh, who was the director of the National Conservatoire of Music. He was one of the very few non-Jews who, despite grave danger to their lives, helped the Jews and, in this case, saved the girls.

When the synagogue was filled to capacity all those there were taken to the forest and killed. I never saw my Aunt Annia and Mascha again and I could never find anyone who could tell me where they had been murdered. A family wiped from the face of the earth – without trace – in the space of one month. I was 12 at the time but realized only a miracle could save us now.

Every day, Jews with little bundles in their hands were herded through the streets like bewildered animals to their place of destiny – the ghetto. About 30,000 Jews eventually assembled there, rounded up from all the villages around Dvinsk. Not a single Jewish soul was knowingly left outside.

Everybody was made to wear a yellow Star of David on the back and front of their clothing. Walking on pavements was forbidden. The ghetto, an old burnt-out cavalry barracks, was situated just beyond the town in the suburb of Griva. Griva was the original part of the city, having been established in 1257, and took over half an hour to reach walking across open fields.

The ghetto looked like any other medieval military stronghold. A huge stone entrance about 20 feet high, with walls 3–4 feet thick, formed a tunnel about 40 feet long. An embankment ran from either side of the gate forming an enclosure that contained a long stone building divided into sections. To the right of the yard was a section housing the German Commandant Zaube and his officers. German guards patrolled the embankment.

There was a sentry box to the right of the gate on the edge of a depression about a quarter of an acre in extent, which had been an old cemetery. The first thing we saw when we were brought to this forbidding place were people, masses of people, packed so tightly together that they overflowed onto the embankment and over the graves.

Because my mother and I had arrived in the ghetto together with the wife and daughter of Dr Magid, who was considered a privileged person because he was the military dentist to the German military, we were given somewhat better-than-average treatment. To accommodate us, the German Commandant must have forcibly removed some unfortunates to place us in a more substantial corner of a relatively undamaged barrack. The overcrowding generally was horrific. I guessed that the ghetto was crammed with at least three times more people than it was ever meant to accommodate. In the heat of summer, thousands of people were crowded together with hardly any sanitary facilities, no food, and only one or two rusty taps for water. At least the warm nights were an

The Ghetto

advantage to people who had to sleep outside in the yard.

The overcrowding was not to last long. In the first week of our arrival an announcement was made that all the old and sick people were to be taken to a special place where they would be cared for. Within minutes there were so many volunteers that queues were formed. Any other place would be better than this. They were all happy to go. As a result the ghetto had a lot more breathing space.

A few days later, a similar offer was extended to parents with small children. Again, the flood of people who wanted to go was enormous. Even people who did not have children tried to get in. Everyone who wanted to go was taken. In a day or two the rumours began. Someone heard from non-Jews who lived on the outskirts of town that for a day and a night there had been shooting and no one had been allowed to go there. Slowly the rumours became fact – there were definitely fresh mass graves! But even then, people would not believe it. It could not happen! How could innocent children be shot?

On 29 July 1941 a small military detachment of high-ranking officers arrived early in the morning. People were waiting in anticipatory terror, to see what would happen. It was announced that because the ghetto was becoming very crowded, and especially since elderly people were finding it hard to sleep in the open, all Jews over 60 would be taken to another ghetto. This would be in the barracks of the old summer military hospital, not far from the fortress.

Seven kilometres from Dvinsk was the Medgziem Forest where, in 1883, Professor Pliater Silber opened a health resort. On the border of this forest was the oldest part of Dvinsk, the old Forstadt. Between the Forstadt and Medgziem, a railway line runs from Dvinsk to Riga. Not far from this point is the Medgziem railway station. Close to the station was the summer military hospital, or health resort, of the local garrison. Those who lived in this area remember the multi-coloured buildings and the sun shining on the garden where many exotic plants abounded. This would be luxury indeed, after the squalid conditions in the ghetto.

Although rumours had trickled into the ghetto that the elderly people were no longer alive, nobody believed this was possible.

To Forgive... But Not Forget

On 2 August 1941, the ghetto yard was once again full of soldiers and policemen. Their story now was that as autumn was approaching, a separate camp was being established to accommodate the people from the smaller villages. Only Jews from Dvinsk, Griva, and Lithuania would remain in the ghetto.

The killers were not in a hurry, allowing those responding to gather all the meagre belongings they had managed to save from home. To further emphasize their sincerity, and to fool people into trusting them, they announced that the well-known Dr Gurevich was to accompany them to the new camp, in case someone became ill. This additional information calmed the crowd. A long line of people, escorted by a strong contingent of security police left the ghetto. Through the window, people could see the column of marchers trudge past the bridge, and turn left to the Medgziem Forest. Doubts began to creep in. Were they approaching life or death?

Initially the marchers were brought to a field bordered by a barbed wire fence, and only afterwards driven to the place of violence. Dr Gurevich saw the trucks carrying lime to cover the dead bodies. He witnessed this bloody *Aktion*, and was stunned.

Dr Gurevich managed to escape and made for the farm of a non-Jewish patient of his. Here he was safely hidden. After two months the farmer took the doctor to Riga, where he sought out the ghetto, reasoning that it would be impossible to fulfil a mass *Aktion* in a big city. Here he met a man by the name of Yakob Rassen. In memoirs written after the War, Rassen reports this conversation with Dr Gurevich:

> I saw everything. I heard screams, and the moaning of the suffering people. Some of them were fighting like lions to save their wives and children. They were heroic people. I saw many betrayed Jews who were wounded, bleeding profusely, but they still threw themselves onto the killers, and with bare hands, and stones, wounded more than 20 of them. Some they smothered, and pulled into the graves with them.*

---

*Report in *Jews of Daugavpils*, a book published in Russian by Yakob Rassen, where this quote from Rassen's memoirs appears (Daugavpils: Gregory Nemtsev, 1993). Translated by the present author.

The Ghetto

After the War it emerged that some of those who died by the hands of these Jews were Latvians who helped with this operation of mass-murder.

To look younger than his 70 years Dr Gurevich always tried to appear fresh, and stay active. However these attempts at preservation were futile. Nearly two years later, on 28 July 1944, in another bloody *Aktion* in Riga–Kaiserwald concentration camp, he committed suicide by taking poison. I heard much about Dr Gurevich after the War. I remember him very vividly as he was our house doctor and much respected. He was renowned not only for his medical prowess but as a dapper gentleman who used to dash from patient to patient in a beautiful carriage with an elegant chestnut horse driven by a dignified and friendly coachman.

The quality of life in the ghetto continued to deteriorate. Daily fear and a deep anxiety brought on by the terror of imminent death caused intense mental stress. Most people found it difficult to resign themselves to continuing horrors particularly where some of their loved ones were still alive with them, but could be snatched away at any moment by an *Aktion*. To the remaining leaders it was obvious that life must be encouraged to continue. To strengthen the survivors' morale and physical health it was necessary to somehow establish essential institutions.

First of all a hospital was organized. It consisted of a few rooms, with some beds and a dedicated staff. I read after the War that these dedicated people, most of whom were subsequently killed, were doctors Judin, Damje, Goldman, Rosenblum, and midwives Shmuhskin and Kats, with nurses Milman and Zaltzman, together with a few others on a part-time basis.

They worked hard. Pesia Zaltzman survived and wrote a slim book in Yiddish, in which she described how my mother had helped her to remain alive particularly when she became critically ill and nearly died during the sojourn later in the Kaiserwald camp in Riga. She specifically mentions the food scraps my mother would give me to bring her after dark, remembering: 'This little, miserably thin girl would tug me by my toes and hand me whatever she had.'

According to the ghetto rules, Jewish women were not

allowed to get pregnant. If they did, they would be liquidated. To save these pregnant women the doctors did what they could, under the circumstances. Apart from this, the doctors had to hide dangerous illnesses, against which the killers had their own 'methods'. Alternatively the doctors protected people with false diagnoses to keep them out of the *Aktions*. There were people everywhere, more than one to a bed, on the floor, under the bed, in every space. In the corner of the hospital was a pharmacy, under the management of Shmuel Vovsy. A few pharmacists secretly brought medicines from the town. Dentists were also available but the standards of their services were very rudimentary as equipment and medication was almost non-existent.

From the beginning, the chief of the hospital was Dr Knoch, who had a private clinic in Daugavpils in pre-War days. He was killed in one of the first *Aktions*, and replaced by the well-known surgeon and gynaecologist Yeshue Damje. However, he was eventually called to the gate of the ghetto, arrested, and never returned.

After the first *Aktions* the number of orphans in the ghetto was growing more quickly than mushrooms after rain. An orphanage was opened in one of the barracks. The babies were carried in nappies and placed in a separate room. The supervisor was Wovsi Shtorch, the daughter of the chief executive of Bank Avkaam – Elie Shtorch. In one of the *Aktions* the whole orphanage was liquidated, together with the supervisor. I remember some time before, going to the orphanage and begging my mother to take one of the babies. Little did I realize at the time what a hindrance that would be for her.

The local 'government' known as the *Judenrat*, was organized and headed by an engineer, Misha Movshenson, who was known to be a dandy. His father was a wealthy man, and was killed by the Russians when they occupied Latvia. Another man, David Selikman, was offered a position on the committee, but he refused, saying he didn't want to serve the killers, and betray his people. He too was killed in one of the early *Aktions*.

The poverty and hunger in the ghetto grew from day to day. The only available food was sour cabbage soup, consisting of water and rotten leaves. The individuals sent to work outside the ghetto were considered fortunate. They were able to make contact with non-Jews, and acquire some extra supplies. The lucky ones able to work outside had first to be issued with *sheins* (work permits).

On 17 August 1941, the police arrived and announced another version of an *Aktion*. They needed a lot of workers to dig beetroot. People were divided into left and right columns, and led away in the direction of Medgziem. When they reached the fields they saw freshly dug graves and executioners with guns. The killing of Jews provoked a protest from some of the Latvian non-Jews. Some even tried to help where they could but – as the danger was great – these examples of humanity were few.

To ease the impression of the 'New Regime' the *Daugavpils News* newspaper wrote an article about the conditions in the ghetto, stating that these were not bad at all: 'They have their own police of six people. There is a shoemaker, a dressmaking establishment, a hospital, a dentist, and a clinic with eight doctors and nurses. So, if the Jews complain, it's their own fault.' It is recorded that between 13 July and 21 August 1941, 9,012 Jews were murdered in Daugavpils. (These figures do not include the people murdered in the prison.)

The next few weeks were quiet. There were no more people sleeping in the yard. Occasionally, small groups of people, men and women, would be brought into the ghetto from some hiding place, or little village. Everyone would rush out to see if any of their relatives were amongst them.

The stables underneath the building – originally intended for horses – were now occupied by people. Hundreds of small fires burned with a little pot or a tin between two bricks on either side, to enable people to cook whatever they could lay their hands on. In many cases, the closely guarded tins or pots contained only a few potato peelings. There was some sort of order. Jewish police had been appointed. A kitchen, a clinic of sorts, and a small sewing establishment, were somehow organized.

Although by now everyone was able to sleep inside, there were still many people who slept on the floor, including my mother and me. The others established makeshift timber bunks. Groups of people were taken out of the ghetto to work under guard. Going out to work had a few advantages. First, one could hear news from the battlefront. Second, it was sometimes possible to exchange clothing for food with the non-Jews, or simply beg for some. The working people were issued with work permits. Life was starting to take on some kind of order, but this was not to last long.

One morning, more than the usual number of guards appeared on the embankment. High-ranking officers were walking up and down the yard surveying the ghetto. The Jewish police were summoned.

We were all tense and frightened, expecting the worst. Mothers cuddled their children, pacifying them. Suddenly we heard shouting. *'Raus! Raus! Raus!'* German SS men with rifles were chasing people from all the buildings into the yard. No one knew what was happening. When everyone was outside, the officers started a sorting out process – 'You to the right; you left! Two to the left! Five to the right!' At last the mass of people was divided into groups. We sensed death, but no one knew which side was death and which life. The German officer who was in command appeared to be enjoying himself enormously. He was obviously revelling in his power over his victims. As my turn to stand before him approached I looked up into his perspiring face, pleading silently with my eyes, He was almighty! My life continued only at his whim. His hand moved; I was waved to the left group.

My mother was also allocated to this group. My room-mate had been separated from her mother. She had been sent to the right, and her mother was with us. How frightened she looked! She was too drained to cry! There weren't any more tears. My heart throbbed like a drum inside me. I waited...It was so still that I imagined I could hear other hearts beating, and then the other group was surrounded by the SS men and led away. I took a deep breath and pinched myself to make sure I was still alive. Darting glances between the groups were exchanged. One still had doubts. Perhaps they were being taken to work...perhaps, perhaps.

We stood for a moment in silence, stunned. Then almost at once, the wailing of the bereaved mothers began to envelop us. 'Oh my G–d! What has happened?' We returned to our

The Ghetto

rooms in deep distress. They were half empty. We had all the space we wanted; yet we still clung to our little corner. There was no talking. All that could be heard was the sound of sobbing.

After an hour of so, hesitant movement became noticeable. Routine was slowly resumed. We queued for the scraps that passed for food, went to the toilet or fetched water. We even began enquiring as to who had gone, and who had remained. Smoke arose from the stables as the sad little fires were lit once more. Life stealthily, almost regretfully, resumed.

My mother discovered that people with work permits were not taken. We were just lucky to be in this group. We survived this one of many selections. From that day on, my mother had only one goal: to get to work, and to obtain a work permit.

A group of ten women were needed to wash and sew for some German soldiers. My mother was one of them. While I remained in the sewing circle in the ghetto, she went out daily to work and soon obtained a yellow *shein*. This gave her a feeling of security – for the time being at any rate. Meanwhile, I was to enjoy a chance of going to the sewing circle. A wonderful, elderly lady, who had a beautiful castle-like villa next to our dacha at Stropi, was in charge. Many a long-gone day had I spent in her villa, playing with her grandchildren who came from Czechoslovakia for the summer holidays. She used to do the most beautiful embroidery and made little flowers out of bits of material. To this day, I remember a little black velvet pouch she made, embroidered with flowers. I was at her beck and call. I loved to watch her.

During October and November of 1941, rumours again started to circulate that graves were being dug. People were trying desperately to go out to work. *Sheins* were being traded for gold, bread – or lives.

One day whilst at work, the women in my mother's group were told to return to the ghetto early. They knew this might be the end... The women decided to ask the Chief of Police for whom my mother worked, and who appeared to be a little more human than the other officers, to issue special *sheins* to them. It was agreed that my mother would be the spokesman. When he arrived, she rushed up to him and begged him to save them and their children, because she had heard they were all going to be killed. He was taken aback at the fervour of her appeal, thinking perhaps that she was going to try to kill him. He commanded her to make a list of the names of the women and their children in the group to give to him. The group then returned to the ghetto, knowing that it might be their last day, but hoping that the *sheins* would save them.

As they reached the ghetto gates it was clear that an *Aktion* was in progress. The guards opened the barriers and hustled the group in. Trying to avoid the open parade area where the selection of the doomed was taking place, they found themselves confronted by a distraught group who were running about helter-skelter declaring they were seeking means to commit suicide. My mother confronted three young boys whom she knew and asked them whether they seriously contemplated such a useless death. They looked startled, whereupon she suggested they together find a hiding place under a nearby roof. This they somehow succeeded in doing by guiding my mother to prevent her from slipping as they climbed into the rafters.

On the second day of the action it was clear to my mother and those others in the roof that the panic below amongst those still being sorted was increasing. By then everyone knew what to expect.

It was final! The SS made doubly sure that no one was left behind in the rooms. Mothers had tried to hide their small children in pillows under beds. I cannot get over the fact that the little children did not cry. It was as if they knew that a cry would mean death. In moments like this there was not even a whimper. In the yard, one could cut the atmosphere with a knife. Everyone knew their last moment had come. The sorting continued. This time people with red *sheins* were called up. Red was the colour of life that day. Then they started calling out the names of my mother's group, handing them the red *sheins*. My mother's name was called again and again, but she did not come. Eventually, she appeared looking dreadfully dirty and dishevelled. She rushed up to be handed her **life** – a red *shein*. She later related how the boys she had been hiding with were afraid that if they let her go they would be discovered and had tied her up with rope. After pleading with them, in desperation they had released her.

1. Maja's Russian school in Dvinsk.

2. Hebrew school class, taken in 1938. Only three pupils (marked) survived the Holocaust.

3. Picture taken at Maja's birthday party in 1939. Maja is standing top left next to her cousin, Masha Zarch and her second cousin, Rosa Magid, both of whom were killed. Bottom left is Maja's best friend, Eta Maurin; who was sent to Siberia in 1940.

4. Petronella Vilmans, Maja's devout Catholic Nanny, taken in 1956. She is honoured at Yad-Vashem, in Israel, as a righteous Gentile.

5. Mr and Mrs Zarch and Maja, 1936.

6. Riga street, Daugavpils taken in 1992. The corner shop with the large window was one of Mr Zarch's shops before being nationalized by the Russian government.

7. A synagogue in Daugavpils where Mr Zarch worshipped; it was here that all the Jews were brought together to be killed.

8. The Citadel. On the right of the picture is the building where Maja and her mother lived.

9. The Citadel workshop.

10. Abe Kotzen, a Russian Jewish soldier who warned Maja and her mother not to return to Latvia. Thanks to his assistance they escaped from the Russian zone to the American zone.

11. A group of camp survivors who worked for the Russian Army in Koshalin in 1945–46. Maja's mother is on the far left of the group, and Maja is second from the right.

12. Maja's marriage to Sidney Abramowitch in 1950. Left to right: uncles David and Leon; Maja's mother; Maja; Sidney; Sidney's parents, Ethel and Eias Abramowitch; and David's wife, Lola.

13. Breakfast in Riga with friends. Left to right: daughters Karen and Diana; Mulia Slov (who met the Abramowitch's in Petersburg, and last saw Maja in 1937); Maja; and Sioma Spungin.

14. My family. *Left to right*: son Roy; daughter Karen; niece Shelley; daughter Diana; nephew Martin. *Bottom row*: husband Sidney; son David; and Maja 1998.

15. Memoria Day in Pagulianka Forest where the Jews from Daugavpils were murdered.

16. Granddaughter Kim Smullen at a memorial service at the Johannesburg Cemetary in memory of victims of the Holocaust.

The Ghetto

I managed to survive this dreadful event because of my mother's foresight in having made the arrangement with Dr Magid's wife to take me in as their daughter in an emergency. During the *Aktion* she had sought me out and saved me for 'life'.

My friend, Dina Muravina, who was a year older that me, survived this *Aktion* in a very strange way. Her mother and sister had been sent to the right, whilst she, together with the family she was with and by whom she had been saved on previous occasions, had been sent to the left. Dina was sure that the group her mother and sister were in was the one to be killed. On impulse she rushed over to them, preferring to die with her mother and sister. As it turned out, the other group was led away and Dina with her mother and sister, survived, the last of a large devoted family of which the father and two brothers were killed during the early prison murders.

Those were terrible times. Another selection took place the next day. From every corner there was wailing. To add to the dreadful mood in the ghetto, within a day of the selection, a woman returned as if from the dead. She was hysterical and uncontrollable. When she eventually quietened down, she told us that she had been in the group which had been taken for slaughter. The group was loaded into black canvas covered vans. They were taken a few kilometres beyond the inhabited areas and off-loaded in a stony field. The order to undress rang out, and after the clothes were neatly arranged in piles, they were lined up on the edge of newly deepened ditches. A troop of soldiers appeared from behind the vans and the shooting began. She had fallen into the mass grave and had been taken for dead, but had managed to climb out from amongst the corpses during the night and had returned to the ghetto. Poor soul – she was shortly to go through the whole thing again; this time never to return.

How well I remember another occasion when a woman in our room came back from work and could not find her son. For days she walked around, a woman possessed, talking to her son's winter hat, clutching and kissing it.

The ghetto had again been emptied by death. There was space for all to now sleep on the woefully inadequate bunks. Mrs Magid and her daughter, Rose, were somehow permitted to leave and join her husband in town. All the people were now allocated to the part of the ghetto that was not damaged during the original bombings. Because there were only a few thousand left, all of us could be accommodated in the better buildings which were warmer and even had windows. With the nights getting colder and not enough blankets, this was important. Each dormitory was now fitted with long wooden bunks down each side where about 50 people slept. We were in the last room. My bunk faced the door that led into the passage.

Amongst our room-mates were our old neighbours, Mrs Silina, her daughter Chava, and Chava's younger brother, Yasho, as well as Mrs Bravo, who had a beautiful daughter Mira of 18 or 19, a woman with a retarded girl, and others I cannot recall. My mother went to work every day. I can just imagine how worried she was about leaving me behind, especially as I had become desperately ill.

Just before the War I had had a severe attack of appendicitis. It was decided that I should go to Riga for an operation, but the outbreak of war prevented this. Now, in the ghetto, the appendicitis together with jaundice, struck again. But perhaps because of the stringent diet, I eventually recovered without any serious after-effects.

After a while, my mother and her group were transferred to another place of work – the Soldatenheim. This was a canteen for soldiers, attached to a large building in the centre of town, containing a hotel, theatre, confectionery and a department store. My mother and the other women worked in the hotel kitchen that was run by a Latvian who was an acquaintance of my father. They cleaned the place, worked in the kitchen, washed the dishes, and were happy to bring back all the scraps of food they were able to collect. We were fortunate in not having to depend on sauerkraut soup, which was the only item on the usual 'menu'. In addition, we were eventually issued with ration cards that enabled us to receive 100 grams of meat once a week, a tablespoon of sugar every second day and some margarine.

A few of our group still attended the sewing circle. Sometimes, however, I would go with my mother to her place of work. Because my father's friend appeared not to notice

The Ghetto

me, my mother gave him my father's gold pen that she had managed to save.

Winter was coming. The Germans were advancing deeper and deeper into Russia. Their armies were capturing thousands upon thousands of Russian prisoners. We saw them everywhere: exhausted, bedraggled, and hungry. Occasionally a few words would be exchanged between us. Neither could offer the other any words of comfort. We came across many hundreds of them lying dead under the cover of snow when we were going back and forth from the ghetto to work. They died like flies and no one seemed to care.

One Sunday we were suddenly ordered into the yard. Panic broke out. We were all out in the yard, terrified, when an announcement was made: 'You are about to witness what happens to a woman who wants to hide her Jewishness.' A beautiful blonde woman was brought out with a noose attached to her neck and publicly hanged from a prepared scaffold.

We were overcome with horror. This was Minna Getz who was a friend to all of us though – at 18 – she was already considered old by me. Her only crime, that she had been found walking in a city street by a Gestapo soldier with her shawl covering her yellow star. She was left hanging for a number of days, to drive home the point that you dared not hide your 'Jewishness'.

This was not an isolated instance of cruel murder. Some time later Chaya Meyerov was seen exchanging a length of material, which she had managed to hide, for a kilogram of flour at the gate of the ghetto. She was observed by a soldier, apprehended and publicly hanged during a bitter snowstorm. I also remember a woman called Masha Schneider being brought into the ghetto one winter morning. She was hanged with much weeping among the horrified crowd of women who were forced to stand in the bitterly cold biting wind to watch the retribution meted out for living 'outside' with non-Jewish documents.

In subsequent research in the Dvinsk archives long after the War, it was discovered that on 11 November 1941, immediately after a particularly murderous selection, *Obersturmführer* Günter Talbert, Commandant of the Dvinsk police, wrote to the Area Kommissar of Dvinsk requesting that the remaining Jews still living in the ghetto or ostensibly still working for the German war effort be 'got rid of'. Not only was Talbert responsible for the killing of the Jews of the Dvinsk area but also of many other areas in Latvia. Documents in the archives indicate that in January 1942 he ordered the killing of 47 civilians – men, women and children – in the village of Barsuku.

After the War, the whereabouts of Talbert remained a riddle. It subsequently transpired that he had no intention of hiding. Nor did he change his name or appearance as so many others accused of war crimes had done. He lived in Düsseldorf where until 1965 he was chief of police. What an irony! Twenty years after the War, when searchers eventually found him, he was not even detained – his new wife paid bail of 100,000 DM for his freedom. The matter came to what appeared to be a token trial. In spite of the written evidence of the many who claimed to have witnessed the murders, he was acquitted.

Cases of typhoid were often reported and now we were struck by an epidemic. In January 1942, the ghetto was declared a quarantine area and was closed for the three remaining months of the winter. Conditions deteriorated dramatically. There was no contact with the outside world. Outside workers, including my mother, remained in town and were housed in special dormitories during this period. These became known as 'The Small Ghetto'. It became difficult to survive on the rations, and without my mother's ration book, which had remained with me, I would have suffered even more.

People walked about like shadows waiting for something to happen. Death was the only solution. During my mother's absence I wandered about, a lonely anxious girl seeking a modicum of comfort from my mother's remaining friends.

Every second Sunday the people working in town were allowed to come to the gate of the ghetto and see their relatives. The Sunday my mother was supposed to come she was not there. My anxiety grew with every intervening day. After a month had passed I was called to the gate one Sunday. There, I joyously saw my mother again. She, together with a

The Ghetto

few other women, had been allowed to briefly return with a small gift of food. It was a miserably small parcel but probably a lifesaver. Subsequently my mother was able to occasionally repeat these brief Sunday visits, bringing me those important scraps of extra nourishment. Despite these efforts I began to suffer badly from malnutrition and eczema. Lice and dirt were affecting us. Our only means of washing ourselves, and our bits of ragged clothing, was in the cabbage soup or coffee. To wash clothes in this sort of liquid was not too bad, but to wash one's hair in sour water is another matter. I was covered in boils; the smallest scratch would turn septic. My nights were spent scratching and my days looking for lice. My burning skin just hung from my bones. I was sick and alone – a child of twelve.

At that time, without any explanation, I began to have terrible premonitions about my mother. I went to my friends, crying, and told them of the feeling I had that something had happened to her. They did their best to pacify me, but I was inconsolable. Then our room-mate, Mrs Bravo, was called out one night. Everyone was envious. They said she was lucky because they thought she had been called out for work.

The previous Sunday I had gone to the gate as usual but my mother did not come. I was certain now that something terrible had happened to her. That fateful night I lay awake and was overwhelmed with foreboding. Towards dawn, the door at the far end of the corridor creaked open and a bent figure entered. The silhouette of the dark figure with a shawl around its head staggered closer and closer until it stopped in front of me. It was my mother. Her face was swollen out of all proportion to its normal size; her eyes were black hollows. I was shocked. Could this really be my mother? Only the voice was hers. As shocked as I was by her condition, she was no less horrified by mine. Everyone woke up. She told them her story.

In the Soldatenheim there was a non-Jewish woman who worked with mother. She was a friend of the Bravos, and had their gold and silver in safekeeping. When she discovered that we shared a room with Mrs Bravo, she occasionally put something in my mother's parcel for her. On that particular Sunday, she included a letter in the parcel telling Mrs Bravo not to despair because the Germans were suffering great defeats and their time was running out. She must not lose heart. The parcel was intercepted on arrival at the ghetto, and my mother was arrested and taken to a police cell. They beat her and interrogated her to reveal the sender's name, but my mother would not tell them. She said she did not know the woman who had given her the parcel; she had never seen her before. All to no avail.

She was approached from the back and beaten with a rubber hose. A heavy book was placed on her head and then struck with a hammer. All the time they threatened to kill her. She cried to the Chief, 'You want to kill me because I am Jewish and took a piece of bread to my starving child in the ghetto. Would not any Gentile mother do the same?' He never replied. Instead he stopped beating her, ordered her to face the wall and started shooting all around her.

Her only prayer was that I would survive. Suddenly, a bell rang and a soldier came in. He led my mother away to a cellar. The walls of the cellar were covered with ice; rats the size of cats ran around. She thought to herself: 'Am I alive or dreaming?'

A day later, a Latvian girl who was obviously from the police, came into the cellar with a small parcel. She began talking to my mother and offered her a piece of bread and lard. She asked my mother if she knew of any communists. My mother declined to accept the bread and lard, and told her that she knew of no communists. Later that day my mother was removed from the cellar. A Latvian officer in the corridor said to her, 'Kneel down and kiss my boots.' She reluctantly bent down as he prepared to kick her. At that moment a German passed and stopped him. She was again taken to the torture cell, where the book and hammer routine was repeated. She felt that she was losing consciousness, but knew that they would shoot her if she permitted herself to do so. She was again returned to the filthy rat-infested cellar. In the evening, her inquisitor appeared again, but this time smiled and told her that she was being taken back to the ghetto. She was now certain death awaited her. In her tortured, bruised condition, hardly managing to drag her feet, she was led towards the ghetto. Not a word was exchanged between the guard and herself. The thought that he would shoot her as soon as they reached the open field never left her, but get back she did. Mira Bravo knew that she would never see her mother alive again. We eventually heard that she and the non-Jewish friend were brutally shot.

In the days that followed, my mother tried to clean me up and to wash my sores with the sauerkraut soup or coffee. She scratched me gently during the nights. She almost deloused me. Slowly I recovered somewhat to the extent that the burning itch disappeared and no lice remained on me other than on my head.

Within the next two weeks my mother also recovered sufficiently from her hideous beatings to join the 'toilet' *kommando*. Toilet facilities were hopelessly inadequate, despite the fact that we were reduced by half. Keeping the toilets clean was essential to health and therefore survival. No one would volunteer for this job of cleaning, and the Germans used to threaten that if the toilets were not kept clean every tenth person would be shot. To avoid this, my mother organized and headed this *kommando*. Many years later, Dina recalled how my mother helped her to mount the steps leading to the toilet because she was too weak to do so alone after a bout of typhoid. The duty of this *kommando* was to keep this dreadful place as clean as possible by chopping away the frozen dirt with axes. The toilets consisted of a wooden seat about three metres long, with holes cut out at intervals.

The water supply in the ghetto was often cut off. It was then that the little spring in the cemetery was used as an auxiliary supply, but when the snow from the higher surrounding areas started to melt and formed a little muddy lake in this depression, the spring would be submerged. Having no alternative, we used this water for drinking and cooking, even though the graves were below the surface.

Time lay heavy on our hands. Occasionally, Russian planes would fly overhead on bombing sorties. We prayed that the ghetto would be destroyed by them. We felt that there would just be that little more purpose in dying during a raid than simply being murdered for the crime of being Jewish. We knew that we were condemned to die – we were just waiting for the day of execution. We did not live, but existed from day to day.

Towards the end of March 1942, without any notice, the ghetto was reopened. A ray of hope penetrated. My mother returned to work. Once again I was able to accompany her daily to work. Dina and her mother joined us. It was getting warmer. My dear Nanny resumed her long waits in the fields. There she would stand for hours on end until she saw us returning to the ghetto. Discreetly she would hand us a piece of bread or, in summer, a few berries she had gathered in the forest. At work, Dina and I washed dishes and became experts in the art of wiping six or more at the same time. We collected the tobacco from all the cigarette ends left in ashtrays and exchanged or sold it for food.

One day, on our return to the ghetto, we found my Nanny was waiting for us, upset and agitated. She told us she had heard that graves were again being dug. Her fervent plea was that we should convert to Christianity, for she felt that because we were Jews and she a devout Christian, it would be impossible for us to meet in heaven. This deeply religious Catholic woman risked her life every time she met us but, despite this, she never failed to arrive. We agreed to be sprinkled with her holy water. The following evening she was there in the field waiting for us with a little bottle of liquid to anoint us. She baptized my mother and me, said a prayer and gave us both a medallion of the holy Mother and Child. There in the field at night, under the lonely stars, she was convinced that we had become Christians. She was relieved and happy. The next time we met, shortly after our 'conversion', she announced that she had arranged with her uncle, with whom she shared a cottage, for me to come and live with them. My mother agreed and after our next meeting, all having been prepared, I was smuggled from my mother's place of work, without my yellow star, and safely reached my Nanny's house.

She lived in a very primitive, ramshackle wooden bungalow on the outskirts of Dvinsk. The tiny property belonged to my Nanny's aged uncle and was just large enough to have a yard that just coped with our needs. The house itself consisted of the kitchen, a large, high, tiled stove on which I slept at night and hid most of the day. Two small bedrooms housed Nanny and her uncle who seldom appeared. I remember this sojourn as a very hazardous, lonely time.

The Ghetto

After two months the neighbours became suspicious, and the uncle heard people gossiping about a child being hidden by his niece. After a lot of soul-searching, Nanny decided to return me to the ghetto. Whilst I was with her, she told me why she had asked us to convert to Christianity. It was her habit to go to church every day to pray for us and, after hearing the story of more graves being dug, she decided that a very special prayer was needed. She became so engrossed in the prayer that she did not notice the congregation dispersing until she was alone. The priest approached and saw that she was in a trance. He asked what was troubling her. She told him her secret and of her fear for our safety. It was on his advice that she had converted us.

On 1 May 1942 we went out to work as usual. During the day, someone ran into the kitchen and told us that they had seen the terrible black canvas-covered vans filled with people leaving the ghetto. This meant only one thing – another selection. To the Jews of Dvinsk, a lorry with black canvas covers had become a symbol of death. Every time Jews were taken to their deaths *en masse*, it was in these lorries. The news was that the ghetto had been liquidated. By then we had no relatives left in the ghetto, but there were the other women with us who had children, parents, brothers and sisters there. We were all speechless. What was to happen to us now? Evening was approaching and we had to return. We were petrified. We asked the Chief if we could remain for the night but he refused. Dina and her mother decided not to return, and ran to her sister who was working at the Citadel (see next chapter). They spent the night there hidden in the straw.

Not a word passed between us on our walk back to the ghetto. As we were crossing the field we became aware of an oppressive silence. At the gates a drunken guard met us. All over the yard, there were pools of blood, broken bottles and parts of chairs: mute testimony to a last useless resistance. We walked on. Children's bodies lay around, torn in half with the heads smashed in. We were horrified; stunned; speechless. We returned to our deserted dormitories. The ghetto was a morgue. We were afraid to move. A few of us went to the toilet. Inside the toilet we heard voices faintly calling. We looked at each other; we thought we were going mad. We looked around; there was no one there. Yet the voices persisted, urgent, muffled, faint. We stood as though we were rooted to the ground. Then suddenly someone caught sight of faces. Two teenage boys were standing deep in excrement, with only their faces sticking out. They must have stood there most of the day and had reached the end of their tether. We had to rescue them at once – but how? We women could not reach down to them and we had no rope. We ran to fetch some of the men who had returned from work and were as stunned as we were. Eventually they dragged them out. The rest of the night was spent in anguish huddled together, waiting for someone to come for us. We did not expect to leave the ghetto alive. Dawn broke. We stirred. We drifted to the gate wondering if they would let us go to work. They let us out...

Thus, after ten months of hell, the ghetto of Dvinsk died. Virtually all the inhabitants had been butchered, including the council members and the internal police force with their families. Of the approximately 30,000 Jewish inhabitants about 500 survived. These were transferred to the Citadel. Among those miserable survivors were mother and I.

The Citadel

The transfer to the ancient citadel signalled the start of the next phase of our lives. As I glimpsed the ancient walls from afar, the memories of ogres and their castles from my fairy-story books crossed my mind. Were the horrors here to be worse? The complex was founded by the Russian Tsar Ivan the Terrible in 1577 after he had conquered Livonia, as Latvia was then known.

The Citadel was a medieval military stronghold on the other side of Dvinsk from the ghetto. Unlike the ghetto, it formed a self-contained, small, military town approached through a large stone-arched gateway. It had neatly laid out narrow cobbled streets lined with ancient buildings. The original stone church with its twin spires dominated the settlement. Even Napoleon was interested in using it during his advance on Russia, but after a visit, decided to bypass its facilities in the interests of speed.

No civilians lived there apart from the occasional ones employed in some capacity by the Germans. The local garrison was stationed there. There were *Wehrmacht* soldiers, *Luftwaffe* personnel and the SS. We, the pathetic survivors, were billeted in two large buildings. On our arrival there the ground floor was already occupied by Russian prisoners of war in the most primitive conditions. For the first few weeks we shared the same entrance through the yard, and gradually made friends with them. We were united in suffering and often discussed our experiences. Sometimes after work, we would join them in singing their sad Russian folk songs, accompanied by a harmonica. Their recreation time was spent making rings out of copper coins. These rings were exchanged for bread or tobacco. Some of the girls were given the rings out of friendship; others placed orders for them. Each prisoner had his own particular design. Our coexistence did not last long. A new iron staircase was built for our use on the other side of the building. From then on, the only contact we had with the prisoners was through a little barred window under the stairs.

The whole upper floor was divided into three or four large rooms and a few smaller ones, all joined by a long corridor. The rooms were fitted with wooden double bunks placed close together. In most cases no tables or chairs were provided. Each of the large rooms accommodated about 20 or 30 people. One of these became our 'home', shared by many women who remain vividly etched in my memory.

My bunk was next to a girl whose name was Elka. Because of her hairstyle, arranged in a peculiar high bun, she was known to us all as Elka the Bun. She eventually survived. Across the room there was a very lively, attractive young lady whose spirit even the Germans could not break. Her name was Raia Lvov. She was the life and soul of our room and, on many occasions, the source of heated arguments. Although she was killed later, her memory still evokes warm feelings. Another woman was the surviving ghetto nurse Pesia Zaltzman, who had worked so hard with the ill-fated children. Other occupants were Nata and her mother, Madame Adelberg. Nata was a beautiful girl of about 17 with long black ringlets framing her face. Lena Rosenburg and her daughter, Ita, lived near the window. Lena was a teacher. The daughter, a girl of about 17, had a lovely voice and often sang us her favourite song 'The Nightingale'.

A very big woman with a strong face, by the name of Mrs Landau, who came from a prominent family in our town, dominated our room. She was very intelligent, and because of her strong character became our self-appointed spokeswoman. She took care of a sickly looking, highly intelligent boy of about 12, called Sania Voldenberg. His parents had owned a stationery shop in our town, but both had been murdered in the ghetto.

Sania was our 'Minister of Information'. He somehow managed to lay his hands on newspapers, old and new, pulled out of rubbish bins, and disseminated information with up-to-the-minute commentary on political and military events. His opinions were undisputed. Subsequently he too was killed.

The Citadel

One of the smaller rooms near ours was shared by, amongst others, my closest friend Dina, her sister and mother. To this day, although we live a continent apart – she in Israel and I in South Africa – the bonds wrought by the horrors of those days have not weakened. When we reminisce, our thoughts often return to that small room and beautiful Mira Bravo, the daughter of the tragic Mrs Bravo. That girl's saga was so very poignant and especially sad because it involved our senior German overseer, an officer by the name of Fritz Staedler.

He was a tall, handsome man, well built with well-groomed black hair and flashing green eyes. He always moved fast as if in a perpetual hurry. Mira and he fell madly in love in spite of the certain death they both risked if discovered. He spent every spare moment in her room. The love they bore each other was tender, deep and genuine. When he was granted leave to visit his family in Germany, to whom he was obviously devoted, he was always reluctant to spend the time away.

It seemed so strange to us that a Jewish girl could fall in love with a German who, during that time, was a symbol of death to all of us. But it happened inexplicably, even though there could be no fulfilment and no future to this doomed relationship. For us it was a beautiful event, even though it introduced an added anxiety into our daily life. All of us felt an implicit involvement and did all we could to shield the lovers from discovery. He was accepted in the room as one of the family and, during his presence there, two of us were constantly on guard in the passage and at the bottom of the stairs.

Besides bringing an unaccustomed dimension into our drab, precarious existence, he also became a veritable guardian angel. The ever-present danger of being disposed of was acute whenever the volume of work diminished, but Fritz would immediately assure the invisible authorities that in no way could he do with a lesser number of workers. Thus, time and again, he rescued us from death.

During the first few days in the Citadel, a group of us were sent to clear all the surrounding pavements of weeds and grass. The others were divided into two groups. The bigger one, consisting of men and women, was sent to a little railway siding about a mile away to off-load clothing arriving from the battle front. On one side of the railway siding there were a number of warehouses, one of which housed a disinfecting chamber. After unloading the train, we would carry bundles to the disinfecting chamber and fumigate them with deadly cyanide gas. After a few hours, or sometimes overnight, the doors and windows were flung open to allow the gas to disperse and we would transfer the clothes to other warehouses where they were sorted according to article. Those in need of repair would be sent to the sewing department, a building across the road from our lodgings.

Life took on a certain routine. People working on the railway siding usually tried to steal or 'take' articles of clothing and exchange them for food. The other group had the advantage of working under cover in the sewing factory, which in winter and on rainy days was a blessing. The group working in the sewing factory found it much harder to steal because the controls were much stricter. I worked for a while outside with my mother, but then was transferred to the sewing factory where I soon started making little doll's suits for the children of the German officers, and little fur hats that they took as gifts when they went on leave. The dolls were made out of all sorts of bits and pieces but mainly cloth, wire and fur.

Looking back, I wonder at the ingenuity of adapting the most primitive and unimaginable objects and obtaining a rather pleasing effect. The orders for the dolls were coming in so fast that I had to enlist the help of my friend, Dina. We were happy in our work. We did not suffer undue hunger as both our mothers worked outside and 'took' a few things to supplement our rations. The taking was not without great risks, except when Fritz was about. In the sewing factory I also learned how to make slippers out of trench coat material. I borrowed lasts from the shoe repair shop next to us and we sold the slippers. I made a pair for my nanny, which she wore until the end of the War.

Among the other helpers occasionally pressed into service was another dear school friend, Frida Friedman. She was to eventually survive as the sole remnant of her entire family. About 35 years later, in South Africa, I one day received a letter from her informing me that she had arrived in Israel some time ago. She had only just learnt of my survival

The Citadel

through a casual friend and hastened to make contact. It transpired that after liberation and many subsequent illnesses due to the privations in the camps she found asylum in Israel after qualifying as a textile engineer. One illness left her deaf and partially paralysed, but she had managed to find employment. Soon after establishing contact I visited her in Israel but by then she was again too ill to work and was transferred to a home. Some years later she died, broken physically and mentally.

On Sundays we did not work, so that day was spent cleaning ourselves or filling the cracks in our wooden double bunks with leftover plaster of Paris we found in the yard to prevent the bugs from escaping and giving us sleepless nights. Sometimes, we would be visited by people who worked in town and we were in turn allowed to visit them. Mother and I occasionally met Nanny at Dr Magid's rooms in town. A boy named Meishale Kukler, a year or two older than me, would sometimes come and visit me in the Citadel.

He and his mother worked and lived in town. His father was a tailor. Meishale took a fancy to me and when visiting me in the Citadel on Sundays used to present me with an apple, which was a great rarity for us. After his liberation in Germany, when we lived in Paris, he managed to find us and wrote letters to me in the hope of meeting me again. I later heard that he went to Canada and became a doctor. I have never heard from him since.

One night we were awakened by loud shouting – 'Get up! Get out!' Only one thought crossed our minds – 'This is the end.' We ran outside to find the sky turned red by the flames from a furiously burning warehouse at the nearby railway siding. We rushed down to be marshaled by the German soldiers who were ordering the Jews into the fire to salvage whatever they could. Much was destroyed but nobody was seriously hurt in the effort.

Life continued for about nine months without major upheavals. Then one day in late October, a truck full of soldiers arrived at the sewing factory. We watched apprehensively as they went into the office and after a while we were called in and told to undress to the waist. This was something new and we undressed in trepidation.

The office door opened, two of the soldiers came in and one after the other we were injected in the breast, as a precaution against cholera. I noticed that only one needle was used. Although we were very sore the next day, I do not remember any of us developing an infection in spite of this unhygienic practice.

It occurred to me that this episode was not as humiliating as our monthly visit to the public bath in a nearby village for a process of 'delousing'. There, after returning naked from the communal bath we had to approach a soldier seated on a low stool with a little stick in his hand, examining the women's pubic hair for lice. It was a humiliating experience but we eventually became immune to this intended insult.

Christmas was approaching. Dina and I decided to make a little gift for our Chief, named Luckenwald. The two of us were the youngest there and as a result always felt very insecure. We wanted to please him and gain favour in his eyes as our fate depended on his whim. We worked for nights on end, sitting on our bunks, making a tableau of Snow White and the Seven Dwarfs, out of scrounged scraps of waste. Two of the dwarves were sawing wood, two of them were chopping and the rest were busy doing something else. They were all dressed in red with long white beards. It looked beautiful and everyone admired our handiwork. Christmas morning arrived. Dina and I proudly carried the tableau to his apartment some blocks away trying to guess how he would react. Would he give us something for it: perhaps a loaf of bread or a tin of something, or perhaps even a piece of Christmas cake? We were full of anticipation. We knocked at the door and he let us in. We handed him the tableau and wished him well. He returned our wishes by saying, 'I wish you what you wish me.' He must have known what our wishes for him really were! He left us for a few minutes, went into the other room and came back with **one** sweet for each of us. We looked at each other and could have cried with disappointment. So much effort for so little return! We thanked him and left.

At the beginning of 1943, the air raids became more frequent. The trains with clothing were arriving more often too. Our 'Minister of Information' was reporting the retreat of

The Citadel

the Germans. The tide had turned. We could feel the change of mood amongst the Germans and this presented new problems.

If the Germans retreated, would they leave us behind or kill us on the spot? Would they deport us? We were preparing for all the eventualities. Four of the girls were making secret arrangements with the prisoners of war to escape to the partisans. For days on end, the girls would stand on the stairs talking to the prisoners through the little barred window. No one suspected what they had in mind. One morning the window bars were broken and the girls were nowhere to be found. Unfortunately they did not make it; they were caught soon afterwards and shot. A few days later, in reprisal, 12 of our people were taken out and killed. A number of boys in the group were trading stolen goods for guns or any other weapons they could lay their hands on, rather than for the usual bread or potatoes. Unfortunately, one such acquisition led to a tragedy. A boy shot himself while cleaning his gun. Although one of our fellow prisoners was a doctor, the boy could not be saved. All sorts of excuses had to be found to conceal how he had died. The discovery of the real cause could have resulted in death for everyone. For once, being Jewish worked in our favour because the Germans did not take great interest in the cause of death of just another Jew. However, for us, getting rid of the body presented a big problem. It was my mother who, with some other people, buried him during the night in the yard where we lived.

My mother and Mrs Landau were deciding on a hiding place somewhere in town. Mrs Landau's family owned a factory in the suburb of Gayok. The factory had burnt out, but underneath it was a very well-concealed cellar that could provide an excellent hiding place. They went to inspect it, and when they came back decided to start laying-in stocks. From then on, every time one of them went to town they would go to the cellar, which could only be reached by going down a plank as the stairs had burnt away, and carefully hide whatever they had managed to get. Sometimes it would be dried beans, rusks or tinned food. Once, when it was my mother's turn to go, she slipped on the plank and fell to the bottom. She lay there for several hours unable to move. Then, gathering all her strength, she lifted herself up and groped her way out of the cellar. She was very bruised, but fortunately nothing was broken.

We never had the opportunity of using this hiding place but, although we did not know it then, some youngsters had discovered it and made use of it later when they managed to escape as we were being taken to the railway yard to be put on the train for the trip to Riga. One of them was Elka Gever. He survived and lives in Israel. He visited South Africa and told me how this hiding place helped him, and the incredible story of his eventual survival.

Apart from our hideout, many of us managed to acquire poison in the town. Some even had morphine in horse-killing doses. We were not about to give our captors the pleasure of shooting us. My mother managed to get two cyanide pills that we kept in a little glass bottle. All the poisons were obtained with great difficulty in exchange for clothing and deprived us of our extra food. My mother told me how to take the poison, assuring me that it was painless and instant. She would say, 'Just put it under your tongue, that's all...'

Now there were Russian air raids almost every day, and our hopes were rising when unexpectedly they were shattered again. Early one morning, without any warning, we were surrounded by the SS soldiers and ordered to get out. The black vans were outside. We knew what that meant. People started running in all directions, trying to escape. We were hoping to get to our cellar somehow. We panicked and, without giving it much thought, climbed on to the roof. Little did we realize that there we could be seen from all sides of the street, and in no time at all SS men with rifles were chasing us down. I crawled towards the nearest SS man and clutched his legs, begging him not to shoot me. I showed him my bottle of poison and beseeched him to allow me to take it. Instead he swung his rifle and kicked the poison out of my hand, rounded us up and made us join the others already in the vans.

We were taken to the station and loaded into cattle trucks. We had no idea where we were being taken. In spite of the fact that many of us had the poison, we waited to see what would happen. The instinct for survival is so strong in most people that until the bullet hits there is hope. As soon as the doors of the trucks closed, many of the people lost hope and started taking their poison. Dr Rosenblum took out his big ampule of morphine, broke off the top and drank it as if it were champagne; others followed suit. Someone hanged himself in the corner of the truck. No one tried to dissuade anyone from doing any of these things. My mother discussed the matter with me. Perhaps the poison in our bottle would not kill us both – perhaps one of us should take it and be sure of the result. The only problem was that each one of us wanted the other to have the luxury of instant death. As a result, neither of us took it. During the journey which lasted two or three days, all the people who took the poison died except Dr Rosenblum. He woke up the following day, looked around, sighed and said, 'Oh G–d! I thought I was dead. What a pity I did not die.' He went to sleep again, only to wake up on the third day to the stark reality of our arrival in Riga.

This arrival ended a nightmare journey during which we received neither food nor water – a nightmare journey which caused some of us to even envy the dead and dying who were thrown out at every infrequent stop. As it turned out, this was only a portent of things to come.

Riga–Kaiserwald

Riga, the capital of Latvia, the 'Paris of the Baltic States', was a seat of culture. It is said that one of the largest church organs in the world is housed in the 'Domkirche', built in 1204. Yet it is as if every stone in this beautiful city is covered with Jewish blood. Thousands of Jews from Riga and the surrounding area, Germany, Poland, and later Hungary, were brought here to be killed. The reason for this was that so many Latvians welcomed the opportunity afforded them to carry out this grisly task. In 1990, after the trials that took place in Riga, it was officially stated that 80,000 Latvian Jews and 2,000 Jews from Europe were killed in Latvia alone.

On our arrival in this beautiful city on 1 November 1943, we were met by shouting Germans with dogs. The doors of the trucks slid open. Once again the dead were thrown out like sacks of potatoes. The rest of us, who were barely alive, were herded together, loaded onto lorries and taken to the Riga ghetto. The Riga ghetto by then had been almost liquidated, but there were still a few pathetic people there who scraped up some food and drink for us. We were to be there a very short time but the horrors they related to us in matter-of-fact, flat tones of hopelessness, heightened our own deep foreboding. How much suffering could the human mind withstand and how much more hunger could our bodies survive? We were soon to find out.

After spending a few hours there, we were taken to Kaiserwald which, as the name implies, was one of the smartest suburbs of Riga long, long ago. Beautiful villas graced this quiet and wooded place. Now, on the edge of the forest, along the railway line and away from the remaining houses, was this dreadful-looking camp.

Before entering, we were all led into a brick enclosure without roof or floor. People had scratched their names on the walls in every possible sort of handwriting with any objects that could make a mark identifying names of mothers, fathers and children – all in the hope of finding each other. With my hairslide I scratched on a vacant part of the wall: 'Rebecca and Maja Zarch were still alive in the winter of 1943.' This was a holding area until the next stage was ready. From there, we were all sent to the showers where our clothes were taken away and we were given other clothing. We were allowed to keep our shoes. I can only remember the little blue blouse I received, because other items of clothing escape my memory. It was rather lucky we were not given a body search because my mother, like so many other people, had managed to hide a few pieces of jewellery and gold coins. Our names and ages were recorded in files that were then removed. We were given numbers, and from this moment we ceased to be individuals. I was now 68888. My mother was always a few people behind or in front of me. We never stood next to each other, because the chances were that if we were identified as mother and daughter we would be separated. All of us were lined up in front of a large barbed-wire gate. To the left of us was the women's camp and to the right, the men's. Separating the two was a high barbed-wire fence.

In the women's camp were five or six large barracks, each one housing about a hundred people. We were sent to barrack number five. The furnishings in the barrack consisted of a three-layer wooden bunk in the middle, which stretched its whole length. The width of the bunks was just sufficient to enable people to sleep head to head. I vaguely remember straw either in sacks or just loose. I have no recollection of blankets, but at night we put our clothing, including shoes, under our heads. My mother and I slept in the middle section. There were also a few long primitive wooden tables and benches in each barrack. Our first introduction to camp life was the *appell*. An *appell* (roll call) was a somewhat disguised practice of torturing people.

Twice a day we were chased out at lightning speed to line up five deep in front of our barracks. More dead than alive, sick or disabled, rain or snow, we had to stand there until counted, first by our *Kapo* (an overseer – one of the inmates appointed by the Germans) and then by the SS man. Erica, an

SS woman, was in charge of our barracks. She was a rather attractive brunette and always walked about with a cane in her hand, but she had a terrible temper and was feared and hated by all others. On the point of collapse from our long waits, we were allowed to return to the barracks. In addition to the Jewish *Kapos*, Kaiserwald, like many other camps, was 'honoured' to have German criminals amongst its police. Usually they were the ones condemned to life imprisonment or hard-labour camps. The most hated and feared of these in Kaiserwald was 'X'. There was also Max, second in command to 'X' and much less feared.

In our barracks there were also German women prisoners, many of whom were former prostitutes. Their duty was to look after us when we were working in the camps. Their rations were better than ours and they did not work. During shower time they usually took command of us with shouts, whipping and kicking us on a whim. I remember one of them was a midwife who had a habit of murdering the very young. She had been condemned to life imprisonment.

Winter or summer, we were awakened at 4.30 every morning. After queuing for ersatz coffee, the work *kommando* would assemble. Some *kommandos* consisted of a hundred or more people, some of much less, depending on the work to be done. We would stand for hours in groups, waiting until the name of our *kommando* was called out. From there we were taken under guard to the place of work. Waiting like that on a summer's morning was not so bad, but in a winter blizzard, without adequate clothing, it was quite a different matter. The first few days after our arrival we were engaged in work that defies description.

Twenty or 30 of us, including Dina, her mother and sister, were taken outside the camp and separated into two groups about a hundred feet away from each other. Next to each group was a little mound of soil. We were made to take off our jackets or jerseys or whatever clothing was available, put the soil into these with our hands, then run to the opposite mound and empty the soil there. This operation was then repeated by the opposite group.

To keep us up to speed, the guards kept pushing us with their rifles. This we did for a few days. It was very difficult for me to run as I had grazed my knee whilst crawling on the roof in the Citadel before our deportation, and the wound had turned septic. Every morning I would crawl out of 'bed', clench my teeth and bend my knee to let the scab crack. This allowed the pus to drip out so that the pain would be relieved and I would be able to limp about on my swollen limb.

Our next task was to build a road. There, our *kommando* consisted of about 50 women who pushed wagonettes with soil and stone all day long. A few of us were made to clean the bricks. We sat in the middle of a field with a hammer for the entire day. To relieve the heat I got a little tin with water and watered my arms every now and then, little realizing what this would do to me. By the end of the day my arms were covered with blisters that by the next day had all turned septic. I continued to work, feeling very ill, but eventually recovered without any treatment. Sometimes we worked under civilian overseers and occasionally exchanged some of our remaining jewellery or gold coins for bread. My mother still had one gold coin left which she always carried with her. When we were taken to the showers she used to stick the coin to the sole of her foot with a bit of tar. While she was working she always rolled up her sleeve and put the coin into the folds. One day before we returned to camp, she took off her dress to shake out the dust and lost the coin. We were terribly upset when we discovered our loss back at the camp, but the following day as soon as we were at work we ran to the place where she had shaken out her dress and incredibly she found it. You can imagine our joy!

Life in the camp was work from dawn to dusk and queuing for soup and ersatz coffee. Sunday was our day of rest, which was usually spent in delousing ourselves – our main occupation – or sleeping when not called for *appell*. We sometimes had entertainment that was provided for us by one of the inmates, a lively young girl from the Vilna ghetto, who sang beautiful songs. They were usually very sad and expressed our sentiments. Even our camp commandant used to come and listen to them. He particularly liked the one about a little village, which we sang with great feeling. Her lovely disposition and wonderful sense of humour were the only bright spots in our miserable existence.

After working for a few months on the road, we were transferred to harbour work, whilst a large group of people was sent out to live at the place of work at Strassenhoff – a big textile factory – where non-Jews worked in two shifts. The Jews were made to work 12 to 16 hours a day. Dina, her mother and sister were sent there. Amongst the Kaiserwald people this was supposed to be one of the better places of work and was much sought after by the rest of us. But for the majority of the Strassenhoff people it turned out very sadly.

Our work in the harbour was very hard; to reach it we walked for an hour often in rain and cold. I was the youngest person who worked in this group and was often pitied. Once during our harbour work I became very ill for a long period but, because I was afraid to remain in the camp, my mother and the other workers literally carried me on their backs. At work, the German, but humane overseer, would allow me to hide myself during the day. Sometimes he would call me into his office, with the pretext of asking me to make the fire in his little stove or to make coffee for him. There were actually two soldiers that I remember who took pity on me.

The off-loading at the docks was supervised by another German who acted rather strangely but, as we later discovered, was anti-Nazi. Time and again when Mother and the others unloaded a piece of machinery from a ship, he would say 'Let us do something different.' At first he was viewed with great suspicion and got no co-operation from the workers, so he went ahead and committed sabotage himself. Then the Jews gave him a helping hand. He was also one of the very few Germans who, at risk to himself, would bring us soup from the leftovers in the canteen. He used to hide it somewhere and then tell us where to look. I wish I could remember his name. I only knew that he came from the part of Poland that was occupied by Germany and called the 'Polish Corridor'. His name was Polish-sounding so it is possible that his origin accounted for his anti-German feelings.

In the winter of that year we endured terrible hardships. We lined our shoes and bodies with every scrap of newspaper we could find. Any sheet we found was like winning the Irish Sweepstake. I often wondered, given the choice, which of the two pains I would choose – cold or hunger? Experiencing both simultaneously is something beyond description. To this day, I cannot understand or believe that a human can endure so much hardship. How **did** we survive it?

In 1944, a convoy with Hungarian Jews arrived in Kaiserwald. They were bewildered and horrified at what they saw. Until then, the Jews of Hungary had managed to escape the fate that befell most of the European Jews. 'How can one survive this?' was the universal question. To console them we would reply rather sarcastically, 'The first three years are the hardest, then you get used to it.'

To add insult to injury and to humiliate us a bit more, new orders were received in July. None of us was allowed out to work. Instead we were all sent to the showers and our clothes were taken away, including our shoes. The women were examined gynaecologically in case they had hidden their jewellery in their vaginas. Our hair was shaved off and we were issued with prison uniforms and wooden clogs. The uniform consisted of striped underwear, a dress and jacket – also striped. The situation became tragi-comical. When we looked at each other, we laughed. We could hardly recognize one another. We were stripped of all possible individuality – thousands of people all bare-headed, and in shapeless clothes. From our experiences we had learned that there was no limit to how bad things can become. When one believed that one had been taxed to the limit of endurance and just could not imagine anything worse could happen, the Germans would beat us to it. They devised plans to shatter all illusions.

Whilst we were bemoaning our fate, the people working in Strasenhoff had to go through an experience even worse than ours. In addition to having their hair shaved off and wearing those ridiculous prison uniforms, only people between the ages of 18 and 30 were permitted to remain alive. All the others were taken away to be killed. Years later, Dina told me how she lost her mother. Her mother was in the over-30 category and was taken away, but managed to escape and hid herself in a ditch. During the day Germans with dogs discovered her, beat her continuously for a long time and then shot her. We did not realize that this was a prelude to the next chapter of our lives.

Within a few days, on Sunday, 6 August 1944 to be precise,

we were all brought together at the Riga docks and loaded into a boat. There was at least ten times the number of people the boat was meant to carry. No food was to be provided during the journey – just a mouthful of water a day. No sanitary provisions. We were forbidden to go on deck.

On the morning of the fifth day we docked in Danzig harbour. After disembarking, we were left to sit in a field in the scorching sun for most of that day. In the evening we were loaded onto little boats that had been used to carry coal, and put to sea.

Though this journey was short, many of us were seasick. We landed at a long wooden jetty in a small harbour to be escorted to Stuthoff concentration camp. Mercifully, a large number of people had not survived.

Stutthof

We finally arrived at Stutthof, a concentration camp located about 35 kilometres east of Danzig, built by the Germans in 1939. The sight of it was a chilling indication of what was in store for us. On both sides of the entrance were huge mounds of shoes, spectacles and some artificial limbs, bearing silent testimony to what had gone before. The camp was surrounded with a high, electrified barbed-wire fence. None could escape the stench of the crematorium that was kept busy there night and day. Although it turned out that we were to spend only a short time here, it was long enough for me to suffer one of the most terrifying periods of my life. In the first week or so of our arrival we met many of our surviving friends because people were arriving every day from all parts of the Baltic States. A group arrived from Estonia that included some of our Latvian people. The beautiful Mira Bravo was supposed to be amongst them, but she had not survived the journey to Estonia. She died of suffocation in the overcrowded trucks that carried them. I subsequently heard from people who were with her that Fritz endangered himself to make several desperate journeys to see her after discovering where she was. In spite of his deep love, all his efforts to save her failed and they were doomed never to meet again.

In Stutthof, living corpses wandered around aimlessly, their deeply sunken eyes staring into nothingness – souls existing from hour to hour with perhaps only the past as a crutch for survival. For some inexplicable reason when looking back at this camp, I see it in sand-coloured shades like the shimmering Sahara desert. Perhaps this was because of the great heat that particular August and the dry dusty sand on which the camp was built, housing inmates whose bodies, spirits, and clothes could be likened to the scorched, barren earth.

The barracks were overcrowded and often three had to

To Forgive... But Not Forget

sleep in a single bunk. *Appells* dominated our days. To meet the required speed with which we were to line up, we would have to jump through the windows. To receive our single meal we would queue up for hours, only to be given a bit of dirty water from a huge drum with a tin attached to a stick for a ladle. A dry slice of bread was thrust into our hands. Some would look at their food as if it were sacred, afraid to start eating. Occasionally, we would see a man or a woman stuck to the fence, electrocuted. Some felt that they had had enough and deliberately touched the wire; others, seeing their loved ones from the other side would run up to the fence, forgetting about the danger. The reaction from the inmates was almost always the same – 'Oh well; the suffering is over.' For further amusement, the Germans would order a woman to crouch on a narrow bench and make her stay like that until she would faint or drop dead.

After about four weeks at Stutthof, 500 women were called out for work and we were happy to be included. We were all taken to a large barrack and divided into small groups of about 20 or 30. We were to go through a 'medical inspection'. Ours was the first group. We were told to undress and parade naked in front of a long table at which sat about five SS officers. The inspection began. Women who had no scars on their bodies and looked as if they could still do work, were stamped on their arms with a number and told to stand on one side. My mother was stamped. I was stopped and asked my age. I said I was 18. They looked at each other and rejected me. Children always added a few years, while the older ones deducted the four years they had been in the camps. My mother said she was 35. I knew what was in store for me and was panic-stricken. My mother and I exchanged glances. The rejects were led away to get dressed. I dressed as quickly as I could and hid myself under the bunk. The others in my group were chased out. My mother's group was led in to get dressed.

I saw her feet and heard her wailing. I tried to get out but I could not move because the space between the bunk and the floor was too tight. I started calling her faintly as I was afraid someone would hear. At last she heard me. She was trying to locate my voice so I told her where to bend down because I could not get out. She asked the other women to help her lift the bunk. My mother's quick action saved me. The number of the last woman to be stamped was still wet and she managed to transfer it onto my arm. My mother removed her panties and stuffed these into my clothes to make me a bosom and I emerged with the others. The Almighty must have answered my devoted Nanny's prayers for our survival, for in the next group rejects were not allowed to mix with the stamped people. I had cheated death once more.

All the women who had passed the medical were pushed into a small corridor-like room for the night. It seemed that we would have to spend the night standing, for there was not even enough space to sit, let alone lie down. We made a plan. One woman would sit with her legs stretched slightly apart and all the rest would fit together in herring bone fashion. It worked for a while, but going to the toilet presented a big problem. Eventually a few of us managed to get out and we spent the night in the toilet, with me sitting on a piece of rusty tin I found there. In the morning we were let out and led to a narrow-gauge railway siding. We were happy to see the last of Stutthof after our short taste of hell. We were taken to Sophienwald.

Sophienwald

To this day I find it difficult to establish where Sophienwald was or is on a map. To us it felt like heaven after the short journey. In the middle of nowhere, we found ourselves standing in front of a neatly laid out camp unlike any other we had seen. Although fenced on all sides with barbed wire and with the usual high watchtower, the little asbestos huts arranged in rows seemed pleasant. From a distance, it looked like a camp built of cards.

Fifteen women were allocated to each hut. The floor was covered with straw. The sleeping area was demarcated by a plank about 12 inches high placed on its narrow edge. Another plank of the same width was nailed flat on top and served either as a table or bench. A passage about two feet wide was left between the wall and the sleeping area. There were no windows and only a narrow door leading outside. Our hut was divided into two groups. Two-thirds of the women were of Eastern European origin and were looked down upon by the other third who were German Jews or 'Yekkes' as they were called in the camps. For reasons that have no logical explanation or basis, they considered themselves to be much superior to us, and to the last moment of their lives still believed that Hitler would exempt them from the fate of the rest of us. After all, they considered themselves German!

The day after our arrival we started work. We were to lay out an airfield. We worked in the scorching sun with picks and shovels while sweat poured off us. By the end of the day we could hardly recognize each other. Our faces were thickly covered with brown dust which stuck to our faces, leaving only our eyes visible. On our return to camp we were faced with a problem – how to get clean?

No showers were provided – just a single pump in front of the kitchen with no washing utensils whatsoever and 500 women wanting to wash. Our Chief realized our predicament and came up with a brilliant idea. Every day after work we were taken to a nearby lake. After undressing completely, we were made to stay in the water until our overseers, who sat on the bank amusing themselves, allowed us to get out.

We adapted ourselves in a strange new way. The area allocated for sleep was just wide enough for us to sleep on our sides all facing in the same direction. To turn over onto the other side, we all had to do it at the same time – not without heated arguments in the middle of the night. If someone had to leave her place to answer a call of nature, she would have to fight to get back into the row.

The division of rations was another source of tension amongst us. In strict rotation, a bucket of coffee was fetched at five in the morning. Fritzi, one of the German women, whom we disliked, was intelligent but arrogant and never failed to remind us of the wonderful cultured life she had lived at home. Naturally, she was very critical of everyone. One cold, dark winter's morning the coffee had been fetched as usual. In the dark we had reached out for our mugs, filled them with coffee and were warming our frozen hands around them. Fritzi complained that the coffee was cold – something that happened to us only too often. However, none of us found it to be so. We all realized what had happened. In the dark she had dipped her mug into a similar bucket used for urinating during the night. What a reflection on both the coffee and our life! At that time our daily food ration consisted of a loaf and a half of bread for the 15 of us, a plate of thin soup, a slice of *bloodwors*, a tablespoon of jam or a piece of margarine.

What precision was displayed to divide the bread into 15 slices! What care was exercised to ensure that the jam did not stick to the spoon after it was spread on the slice of bread, or that none was left on a jam jar lid recovered from a rubbish heap. How happy we were on the day when we could have an extra portion of soup after a voice from the kitchen would announce '*Nachschlag*' (second helping).

With the approach of the autumn rains and winter we were faced with additional problems. Our striped uniforms were hopelessly inadequate. After repeated appeals, we were issued with pullovers and coats. The Germans must have decided that Jews could do without stockings or should by now have become used to the cold. We wore our pullovers on our legs, using the sleeves for leggings and tying the tops with pieces of string. The coats were given out, not according to size, but simply by one's turn in the queue. To this day, my friends remember my mother by her bright cerise coat, tied at the waist with a rope with a mug dangling from it. Those were her only possessions. In fact none of us had anything more.

I worked with my mother and others in the field until I became ill and was transferred to home duty. This included cleaning the huts and helping in the kitchen – a job envied by all. During the morning, I would have to pump and carry as many as 100 buckets of water to the kitchen to fill the drums in which the soup was cooked. I became an expert at cleaning potatoes and carrots at a speed that could only be equalled by a machine. In spite of the hard work and considering how weak I was, I was one of the luckiest people in the camp. From that day on I knew little hunger, for I could always snatch a piece of carrot or beetroot, or get an extra plate of soup to exchange for someone's tablespoon of jam or piece of *bloodwors*.

On the whole a great deal of bartering went on. A piece of coat cut off at the hem for making mittens or scarves could be exchanged for a ration of margarine. The loan of a needle – one of the most precious possessions of the lucky owner – could be exchanged for a similar ration. The same applied to a comb or safety pin. Threads, pulled from the interfacing of one's coat, were sold by the piece. A safety pin was considered the height of luxury and often resulted in fights when one inmate accused another of stealing it.

My creative urge was fulfilled when I made an oil lamp – an invention only equalled by Edison! On a scrap heap I once found an empty toothpaste tube that I cut in half up to the hard nozzle. I twisted a few strands of thread from the linen interfacing of my coat together and pulled it through the nozzle. The remainder of the thread that now formed a wick, rested on the jar lid that contained a small piece of margarine collected from all the inmates in quantities the size of a thumbnail. When I lit the wick for the first time, it felt as if the Almighty had once again brought light to the dark earth. Until that moment, we had lived in complete darkness from

Sophienwald

evening until morning. What pleasure this little flicker brought – it opened a new chapter in our lives. We could do delousing and some sewing. The 'sewing' consisted of someone cutting off the hem of her coat and trading it for a piece of bread or a few spoonfuls of soup. That piece of off-cut was reworked to become a cap or part of a glove.

When the big frost set in, each hut was provided with a small, round cast-iron stove. What unbelievable luxury that was! Previously our hair had often frozen to the wall during the nights and had to be pulled away by force in the morning. Our clothes would get wet during the day, and often had to be put on or taken off, frozen stiff. Now we took turns drying our clothes by wrapping them round the chimney, and delousing them was done in the same manner. Getting out of the huts in the mornings was also one of the winter problems. The doors would be snowed up and we had to wait until someone dug us out.

Our washing routine was handled so that every other evening when we got our coffee, we would drink half of it and use the other half in rotation for washing our faces or hair and then each part of the body. Then in turn, we would wash whatever clothing there was. I have no doubt that this may sound difficult to believe, but it is the absolute truth.

One day a group of sick people were to be sent back to Stutthof. Amongst them was our compatriot, Schienale Ichlov, from Dvinsk. She survived against all odds, and now lives in Israel with her husband and children. We had no hope of ever seeing her alive again, but we met her by coincidence in Paris after our liberation, where she told us of her miraculous recovery in Stutthof, although not without after-effects.

At about this time a very unfortunate incident took place in Sophienwald. On our way back from work one evening we passed a cart being loaded with potatoes. An unfortunate woman, who ran out of line and tried to grab a potato, was shot dead by the guard. In spite of living daily with death, this incident rocked our improving morale and served to herald new trauma.

The events on the war front could not be concealed even in this remote part of the world. Towards the end of January 1945, the Russians had advanced so far that the Germans decided to move us further away from the advancing battle zone. At first we wondered why the Germans would want to move us. Surely the Russians could not have advanced so far? If they had, surely the mighty German Army would eventually be able to stop them. And, in fact, if the Russians were now unstoppable, surely we poor half-dead Jews were not worth saving?! Little did we realize that far from being spared, our inevitable extinction was intended. As living victims we were not meant to become examples of the evil that even the Germans were afraid to admit to a victorious enemy. Another terrifying ordeal was thus about to begin.

The Walk, Gottendorf and Liberation

I have no idea of the distance we covered during the week of our nightmare march. Every day felt like an eternity. Five hundred starving, undernourished women, unable to drag their feet more than a short staggering pace at a time, formed a dark column of hopelessness. The torture of walking in the soft snow with wooden clogs is difficult to imagine. Foot-high tapering mounds of snow accumulated on the bottom of each sole, turning them into treacherous leaden weights. All along the road we constantly searched for hard objects to scrape off this heavy accumulated burden. Right through the march, our thirst was quenched only by the handfuls of snow we managed to grab on the move.

Whilst passing through little villages and towns we envied every dog we saw. Every single one of us would gladly have exchanged our lives for the freedom and life of those lucky animals. The nights were spent in barns or any other structure that could accommodate 500 women. In fact, anything that had a semblance of a roof was good enough. Our luck was in if we happened to spend the night in a barn full of hay; that was five-star accommodation. A pigsty was a good second best. With this sort of 'sad luxury', many people did not survive the march. When we came across a farmhouse we would beg the people for food and water. They would bolt their doors and close the windows. They ran from us as if from the plague. What puzzles me was the attitude of the Germans – civilian and army alike. They must have known that they were defeated. There could be no doubt about that. The end was in sight, yet there was no change in their behaviour towards us – no compassion whatsoever. Even at this late hour were they so indoctrinated with hatred that they thought it wrong to perform the smallest of deeds to save or ease a human life by giving a bit of bread or water?

Sometimes, to keep ourselves from freezing to death during the night, or when we had a break to rest for a day, we would rub our bodies with snow. That would improve the circulation and we felt warmer.

Towards the end of the week we, the survivors of the big walk, arrived in Gottendorf near the Baltic in Western Poland.

It was obvious that before our arrival Gottendorf had been a German military camp. It was situated just off the main road on the edge of a small lake. It had a very well-equipped kitchen and nearby there were two long mounds of potatoes covered with soil to preserve them from the frost. Although there was a barbed wire fence, it was obvious that the camp had not been originally intended for the extermination of the Jews, as there was no crematorium. But our condition achieved much the same objective.

On our arrival, we found a few hundred emaciated men and women in residence. They were non-Jewish political prisoners and in this camp they did not work. There was no escaping from the fact that the eleventh hour was dawning for the German Reich and with it, new problems. The Germans were saddled with perhaps a few thousand Jews. At this late stage they could hardly shoot us, and there were no gas chambers within reach.

On the roads there was chaos. A continuous stream of refugees was fleeing day and night from the advancing Russian Army. There were comparatively few guards in this camp, but then we hardly needed any. None of us could have run anywhere. It seemed that the Germans had decided that it would not require much effort to starve us to death – we were already on the way. A plate of salt-free soup once a day would do the trick. We would queue up from about ten o'clock in the morning to receive a pitiful mug of dirty water in which, if we were lucky, we might find a piece of potato.

On rare occasions we would even have a piece of horse meat floating in the plate, depending on how many horses had dropped dead on the road in the vicinity of our camp. I remember lining up for soup behind Dina when a potato was dished into her plate. As she moved out of the queue a man grabbed it and before she could even shout, shovelled it into his mouth.

The Walk, Gottendorf and Liberation

To expedite the process the men were made to exercise every morning. A hole was chopped out of the ice in the lake and all the men were forced to dip into the icy water. The 'death' *kommando* worked day and night. They could hardly cope with the corpses. People died like flies. One would speak to a person one minute, and he would just pass out the next. Every morning a few of our neighbours could not be wakened. People could hardly walk. They moved like shadows, holding onto the walls of the barracks to steady themselves. To my horror my mother seemed to be going this way too. I just had to find extra food.

I was lucky. A Hungarian girl I knew worked in the kitchen. I used to wait outside the kitchen and she would run out at great risk and put a handful of dried coffee into my hands. I would go to my mother and we would eat it grain by grain. All the left-overs from the German kitchen, including potato peels, were thrown into the toilets. This precaution was taken to prevent the Jews from getting at them. This did not always work and some of them would manage to reach the potato peels, wash them in the lake and devour them. Our only topic of conversation was food. **If** and **when** we survived, there would be nothing more that we could wish for than just to have enough potatoes and that would suffice for the rest of our lives. The luxury of a bath we did not dare contemplate.

A woman from Vilna who slept on the floor next to us managed to salvage a few potato peels from the toilets. My mother plucked up courage one day and asked if she could spare a few for her daughter, promising her that if we **did** survive we would repay her with a slice of cake for every potato peel. She agreed and, as it turned out, some years later with great joy, we were able to repay her.

The situation in the camp worsened daily. By now the Germans were retreating with great haste and the political prisoners in our camp were released. With great envy and pain in our hearts we watched them run to the gates, waving a piece of paper high above their heads as if it were a flag. Some of them were met by their loved ones. For us there was no such prospect in sight.

Late one afternoon as I was walking towards the ablution block facing the lake, I noticed that the sky beyond was very red. Inside, I heard someone say that the Russians were within a few miles of the camp. We were too weak and despondent to show any reaction. In any event, there was absolutely no point in speculating as to our fate.

That same evening, 9 March 1945, we were told to assemble in the yard. The people who could not walk were encouraged to remain behind, and many did. My mother considered staying, but I begged her to make the effort. Just as we were about to leave the camp, many of us rushed for the mound of potatoes and I managed to grab one. We walked out of the camp and into the night whilst I tried to chew the raw potato. We were led onto the main road where chaos and panic prevailed.

There was no doubt now that the Germans were retreating and they were taking us with them so that the Russians would not find or free us. The German policy of trying to conceal the extent of their murderous depravity concerning the extermination of European Jewry was to be followed to the end. Every few miles we would stop to enable the guards to discover in which direction to drive us. We would take the opportunity to drop down on the snow for a few minutes of rest. We begged them to leave us there on the road in the dead of night. They refused, telling us again and again, 'Do not be hopeful of being liberated.' We would incriminate them too much, and if they could not kill us they would drive us into the sea.

Towards morning, we arrived at a little village. The place was unnaturally quiet and few people were to be seen in the streets. On the road a horse with a cart stood waiting for its owner. A bag hung round the horse's neck, and as we passed I put my hand into it and took out a handful of something or other. I ate it all and remember that there were a few dried lumps mixed into the garbage, which tasted like sweet potatoes.

Exhausted, we all stopped and stood around aimlessly until it was decided where we could rest after the night's walk. There was a barn next to the main road and we were led inside. We cried out for food and water and our overseer went out to a nearby pig farm to see if he could organize something for us. As he left, an officer ran into the barn, jumped onto the horse that was sharing our lodgings and galloped away. We became worried, thinking that he was pursuing someone who was trying to escape. Through the cracks in the walls we saw him disappear into the distance. At that moment we heard planes overhead and a few shots were fired. We looked at each other in bewilderment, trying to decide if this was the end of the road for us when suddenly the barn gates were flung open and we were faced by Russian soldiers with fixed bayonets. Through the gates we could see our guard – dead, and Russian tanks on the road.

We were dumbfounded. This was a miracle beyond credibility. We could not utter a word. It could not be true! Within minutes we were reborn. Our survival was due only to the incredible speed with which we were liberated. For some minutes there was dead silence. Then suddenly the people started screaming, crying and running to kiss and hug the Russians. Many just lay on the hay being unable to move; some did not believe their eyes. Some of the men jumped, or rather crawled, onto the tanks moving down the road to the front. Some went mad, and my friend Fritzi was one of them. Poor soul...she had hung on for so long. Someone flung open the gates on the opposite side of the barn and the mob surged forward.

There was a yard full of German refugee wagons loaded with food that had been left there for the night. Within minutes, we could just see legs sticking out of the wagons as people tried to get at the food in them. My mother managed to grab a piece of bread, but when I bit off a piece, I could not swallow. Someone got hold of a tin and was stamping on it and throwing it against the wall to try and open it. People were completely wild. They were delirious.

After a while, a few of us ventured into the street. People were running in all directions, most of them carrying food. I saw one man with an armful of bread, another running with a bucket of jam and someone else with a whole side of meat. Some ran from person to person grabbing whatever they could. We crossed the road and walked around the corner, still afraid to move away. We were afraid of our shadows. We went into a building and in one of the flats found that food was being cooked, but there was not a soul to be seen. We took a few mouthfuls of food, but found we could not eat. We locked ourselves in a room, undressed, threw our lice-ridden striped uniforms out of the window and put on the clothes we found in the house. After a while we ventured out again. On the ground floor there was a grocery shop and a post office. They were deserted. We took whatever we could get from the shop but found that we could not eat much. We decided to return to the apartment above and spent the night there. In any case, pains in our legs and nausea racked our wasted and exhausted bodies to the extent that we could no longer move. The long walk that had lasted a whole night was over. It was 10 March 1945, the Day of our Rebirth.

Freedom and Flight

People often ask me how would I describe freedom? I have since pondered the question and it seems to be that the only adequate answer would be – take a very young stark naked child, set it in the middle of a vast desert and tell it to go home. That is how I felt about freedom. Which way would I turn as I had no home, no family to return to, and no money? In fact I did not even know where I was. To this day I do not know exactly where we were freed.

Liberation did not signal an end to our suffering. Whilst the few of us lay in a stupor of illness in our requisitioned dwelling, hundreds of thousands of Jews were being barbarously disposed of. We did not know it then, but intensified death marches of victims from concentration and 'work' camps, about to be overrun by the Russians from the East and Allies from the West, were to become one of the most horrible sagas of a cruel and wicked German war machine. In defeat, the beast was undertaking a frenzy of killing as it suffered its own death throes. Historians were to indicate that nearly one million prisoners were to die at this time and not all of them were Jewish.

Liberation, freedom and rebirth were virtually synonymous to us in the next few weeks. Many, however, did not survive liberation. Eating and typhoid took its grim toll. The group of friends who comprised our immediate circle numbered ten women. All of us went down with high fever, lying on the floor of our room that looked like an overcrowded hospital ward. There was no medical attention, but we were destined to survive.

Towards the end of our illness a Russian military doctor, who happened to be passing by on his way to the front, was called in by someone. He examined us in disbelief and said, 'How could you be so reckless as to eat normal food? Did you not know that you should have been on liquids and rusks for at least a month after the starvation of years?' His prognosis was not encouraging. Some of us were still delirious and with fever.

We survived, but our recovery was slow. We looked and felt terrible. At the age of 16 I looked like an old woman. There was not an ounce of flesh on me. When I lifted my arms the skin hung like rags. Once we were on our feet again we had to decide what we should do – which course to take. It was nearly four years since we had been free people. We were completely lost, surrounded by a hostile world with no one we could turn to for guidance. The only advice from the passing Russians was that we should try to move on as soon as possible in an easterly direction, away from the front and towards Russia. This was easier said than done.

The first positive action we took was to get rid of our lice. It was fairly easy to get rid of them in our clothing, because we simply helped ourselves to whatever fresh clothing we wanted. We could walk into any house and help ourselves – they were all empty. The people had fled from the advancing Russian Army. However, it was not so easy to get rid of lice on the body for they put up a dogged resistance in their stronghold – the hair – and it took several intensive paraffin treatments to remove them.

We were still very weak and could only cover short distances at a time. There were no trains and we had no money. Our main source of transport was Russian lorries. Once, while we were travelling on a lorry piled high with straw, we were stopped by a military policeman. While he was examining the driver's papers and enquiring who we might be, someone in a group travelling with us recognized him as one of the *Kapos* from Gottendorf camp and decided it was his chance to get even for the time he had been beaten by this man while queuing for his miserable soup. I remember the delay, but not the outcome of the terrible row and recriminations.

Dvinsk, our home town, was our goal. All of us came from there, and all we wanted to do was to get home for we were hoping to find survivors there. Although we were still very weak, we managed to move slowly from village to town, eastwards. During the nights, and sometimes for a few days,

Freedom and Flight

we would stay in any house that caught our fancy. In this way we encountered some unforeseen problems. The biggest at this time was the threat of being raped by the Russian soldiers. Time and again we would have to plead with them to leave us alone. 'We have had enough,' we would tell them. 'We have just returned from the death camps.' Often it worked because we could communicate with them as we spoke Russian. We were luckier than most of the other inmates, who could not speak the language. Often they would counter with, 'Who liberated you? You subjected yourselves to the Germans – are we not good enough?' I was in such a poor state that even the most frustrated soldier rarely gave me a second look.

At one little village where we arrived exhausted, there was more Russian activity than usual. We decided to rest up for a few days and hung a big notice outside our door saying 'Beware of typhoid – infectious.' We found a very nice, sympathetic Jewish officer, who, when we told him of our predicament, was kind enough to order a soldier to stand guard outside our door for the time we were there. Unfortunately, they soon moved on.

For the first few days after occupying any German town, the Russian soldiers were allowed to do whatever they wished. Although at that time I did not have much sympathy for Germans, I pitied some of them for what they suffered from these men. It did not help to think that they were receiving what they deserved.

Germany was a mess. We travelled through many cities and villages in complete ruins. Clothing lay for miles along the roads. Fields were littered with feathers. There was hardly a house we went into where the mirror or the clock was not riddled with bullet holes. It is hard to believe that Germany recovered so completely, both economically and spiritually, in such a relatively short time.

What also amazed us as we crossed vast expanses of Germany, was the fact that only very occasionally did we come across a German with any feeling of guilt. The standard reply on being questioned was that they did not know what was happening. Did it ever occur to them that there was not a Jew left in the entire country? Yet many, even then, maintained it was anti-German American propaganda. 'If so,' we would ask them, 'why did not the Jews return home to reclaim their possessions?' It is incredible how often their reply was, 'They've gone to America.' Only a small minority of Germans were honest enough to admit they knew what had happened to the Jews but could do nothing about it. It was a fallacy to believe that the whole of Germany was generally starving. Every house we went into was well stocked with food.

Somewhere in the vicinity of Stolp we came to a little town that was completely deserted. We installed ourselves in what looked like a small farmhouse. Chickens, horses and cows roamed about in the streets. We had no shortage of food – the only problem was how to milk a cow. None of us knew except Rachael Zelikman. Her grandfather had a farm and she had seen it done. I do not remember whether we managed to get any milk, but I do remember how much fun we had and how we laughed as she tried to milk the cow. We spent a few days there, and then prepared to move on because the Russians had told us that there was sporadic shooting in the vicinity. We never knew how the front would move and we did not want to take a chance.

We now acquired two horses and a cart but did not know how to handle them and again it was Rachael who came to the rescue. It all looked very simple and we admired her superior knowledge in this field. We loaded the cart with our recently acquired possessions including a bucket hung from the side. It all looked right. With Rachael at the reins we all climbed aboard. She gave the order to move, but nothing happened. She tried again, and with a jerk the horses started off down the road, each one pulling in the opposite direction. She had not realized that they were a pair of matched horses and obviously had to be inspanned in the way to which they were accustomed. The bucket on the side of the cart was squashed completely flat because the horse on that side, for some reason beyond Rachael's control, ran so close to the pavement that the bucket banged against every lamp post.

Eventually, by foot and by horse, we arrived at Koeslin, well known for its Pilsener beer. There were very few civilians to be seen. We approached a Russian officer, telling him of our intentions and of our predicament with the horses. He was extremely kind and offered us lodgings in part of a huge building. We cleaned it out and moved out mountains of clothing and household goods. Within a few days, the Russians offered my mother employment as their cook. The rest of us just rested. It was here that we heard that the War had ended, but not before we nearly all committed suicide.

A week or so before Berlin surrendered an officer ran into our lodgings and told us he had very sad news for us. Koeslin was only 200 kilometres from Berlin. The German Army, which had surrendered, had treacherously started fighting again and had broken through. The Russians were ready for all eventualities – perhaps even a sudden retreat. We were very alarmed but fairly certain they would not leave us behind. 'Oh no,' he said, 'We are not allowed to take civilians. But what is wrong with your horses? You could take them and escape.' We look at one another. Here we were in a German town, with the Russians about to abandon us. There was only one thing left for us to do. We would not allow ourselves to be recaptured. We would commit suicide by jumping from the windows.

However, with the Peace Agreement signed, we finally remained with this garrison for a year. We were transferred to the centre of town where a big co-operative was to be established and all of us were placed in some official position. The idea of this co-operative was twofold. The Russians were to stay in Germany for the time being, far from base, and they needed summer uniforms that would be made in this town. There could also be workshops for dressmaking, watch repairs and shoemaking to cater for the needs of the officers, their wives and the soldiers. We were to organize all this, and eventually it was accomplished in a most unorthodox manner.

With the help of a soldier and a lorry, we 'acquired' at least 50 sewing machines in a few days. We simply walked into any house and took the machine. Most houses had one. In the process we acquired two pianos. A baby grand graced Dina's room – an upright, ours. We now had the machines but there were very few civilians, so again with the help of the Russians, we rounded up German women and we were in business.

My mother was put in charge of the workshop and Dina's sister, Ginda, headed the watchmaking shop. Rachael Zelikman, Gliko Magid and others were allocated other duties.

Dina and I were 'Girl Fridays': we worked in the office, answered the telephones and took messages. One day, when I was on duty in the factory that made uniforms, I noticed that the German women did not work. I reprimanded them and told them what I thought of them in German. They did not like it and one of them turned to me and said, 'Don't be so sure of yourself. In 20 years time we shall have Hitler and Germany again.' We were surprised that people completely destroyed by Hitler's ideas could still hope for another Hitler in Germany.

About this time something unexpected and terrifying happened to me. Our group of ten women had been comfortably housed on the first floor of a house where the ground floor was occupied by Russian soldiers. On the floor above us lived two Ukranian girls who had been sent to Germany during the early days of the War as part of the forced-labour programme. One of these girls was in love with a very nice young soldier whom we all knew.

One day we were visited by a young girl from Vilna whom we had befriended. She was a drifting refugee who had nowhere to go as her entire family had died in the camps. When she left I saw her out into the street. As I returned and entered the lobby to our building I met the nice young soldier coming down the stairs. He appeared in an angry mood, as he must have just had a quarrel with his Ukranian girlfriend. I greeted him, causing him to swing around. Instead of a responding pleasantry he grabbed at me, caught my arm and pushed me under the stairs. He then forced me onto the floor and started tearing my flimsy blouse apart. I tried to push him away as I pleaded frantically with him to let me go. This only angered him more. The door of the apartment where he and his friends lived was slightly ajar. He pushed it open and roughly forced me through, closing the door behind him. He then tried to get my panties off. As at that time elastic was unavailable, they were secured with a knotted ribbon. The more he pulled the more the knot became tangled.

At that point I started to scream at him. Miraculously a passing officer heard the commotion and opened the door. I grabbed his leg and sobbed my heart out. He helped me up while berating the soldier. I tore loose and fled upstairs to my mother, dishevelled and with my torn blouse just hanging. I was hysterical and it took my mother some time to quieten me down and understand what had happened.

The soldier was arrested and court marshalled. Against my will I was persuaded to give evidence at the trial, even though just talking about this event was abhorrent to me. I believe he was punished but we never saw him again.

Ever since my arrival in this place I had been feeling ill. I had no appetite, could not eat and frequently vomited. One of my mother's friends was a Russian doctor, a Major. Mother asked him to have a look at me. He took me to my mother's office where he examined me on her desk and said I had to have my appendix out immediately. He had a cut on his finger and said that if it did not heal by the next day he would ask his colleague to perform the operation.

The next day my mother took me to an all-male military hospital where I was admitted and put to bed. They told her she could leave because the operation would not be performed yet. As soon as she left I was prepared, and the Major's friend performed his surgical magic with a local anaesthetic. He was wonderful to me, talking to me and amusing me right through the operation while two sisters held my hands above my head. The following day my mother came to visit me. She opened the door, looked at me and exclaimed, 'What's wrong? Why are you so pale?' I smiled at her and explained that it was all over.

The doctor, who was a Tartar, spent hours at my bedside, listening to stories of the camps and helping me walk along corridors. The doctor's wife, also a doctor, was Jewish. They became great friends of ours. They had me moved to a ward across the corridor from the nurses' duty room because I was the only female patient. I was treated like a queen. Although I spent two weeks in hospital and had red wine with every meal, I returned home still very weak.

Life took on a certain routine and we were very happy in our work. We made many friends among the Russians and our little community was like an oasis to soldiers and officers alike. All of us spoke Russian, most of us were young and all of us had a lot to tell. We even organized a few dances and musical evenings. However, the shadows of the past coloured all that we did.

To Forgive... But Not Forget

At first, much of our recreational time was spent going from house to house collecting 'trophies', as we called them. We often returned with big bundles of clothes or other items that we would display and distribute to whoever needed them.

One day I went into my mother's office and found her hugging a female major. Both of them had tears running down their cheeks and, with great excitement, my mother told me that this major was Jewish and originally came from Riga. She knew my Uncle Isac's family and in fact was related to my aunt's family, the Beskins. Our friendship was sealed and soon her husband, also a major and doctor, was to play an important role in our lives. But what was more extraordinary was that our friendship was to have the most incredible sequel a few years later in South Africa.

Several Polish Army units were stationed in this town and some of them occasionally came to the factory to have their clothes repaired or to place an order. One of the Polish soldiers was a young man called Fred Gilson, aged 21 and the only survivor of a large family. We became great friends with him and discovered he had broken his arm and had tried to get an army discharge, but to no avail. My mother interceded for him and succeeded in having his wish granted. After that he attached himself to us. This sort of story got around and many people with problems eventually found their way to my mother.

In time, our Koeslin home became a meeting place for Jews from far and wide. Time went by and we discovered more survivors. We extended our enquiries about relatives further afield and discovered that Dr Magid was still alive, but not his wife and daughter Rozetchka. Through him we received our first letter from my Nanny, in which her opening words were: 'My dear Christian friends – my prayers were answered.' Thus we established lifelong contact with her which lasted until that dear soul passed on in 1982, aged 94. At that time she was already too old to live alone and occupied a room in her niece's house in Kraslava, a town about 24 kilometres from Dvinsk. Because of her age she was well known, so our letters always got through and I was even able to send her frequent food parcels without difficulty. I also even managed to telephone her when once visiting Paris, as there was no telephonic connection at that time between South Africa and the then USSR. Even though she was only semi-literate, her letters were richly philosophical and meant a great deal to my mother and me.

When a stately avenue of trees was established at the Holocaust Museum in Israel to commemorate the righteous Gentiles who risked their lives for their fellow Jews, the name of my Nanny, Petronella (Lisa) Vilmanis, was commemorated on a bronze plaque under one of those trees.

While still working with the Russians we heard that a centre for the registration of Holocaust survivors had been established in Lodz, Poland. My mother decided to go there in quest of any members of the family who might have survived. In a few days I received a telegram saying, 'Found Bertha, Franca and Barbara. Uncle Herman and Franca's husband dead.' Finding them had been an incredible coincidence. My mother came to the registering office and combed the lists, but could not find my aunt's name. She was about to give up when she noticed my cousin's name and address on the list. Not knowing the town, she enquired from a helpful official where that address could be located. He informed her that Mrs Chwat, because she was the wife of a Polish officer, lived in a remote part of town allocated to the military wives, and added, 'They do not want to be known as Jews, so be careful.' With the address in her hand and her spirits somewhat dampened, she walked out of the office. As she looked down the street she saw a woman, with a big scarf round her head and wearing men's boots, turn the corner. She caught sight of her profile and it was that of my Aunt Bertha. She shouted at her to stop and rushed up to her. Bertha looked at her with amazement, but said nothing, as she did not quite recognize her still-drawn pale face. My mother's excited greeting convinced her and she reacted with a whispered 'Are you still alive?' Arm in arm they walked to a tramcar and for the next few days, living with Bertha in her flat, she caught up with some of the tragic family story. This story could fill a book, as could that of most Jews who miraculously survived the unbelievable horrors of the German conquest of Europe.

At that time Bertha's immediate family consisted of women only, but of course when the War started in August 1939 it had obviously been different.

To Forgive... But Not Forget

My cousin Franka was married to a handsome Jewish-Polish army officer and they were stationed in Lodz. He was killed very soon after the War started, leaving a young wife alone to face the horrors of German occupation. Soon after the victors started herding the Jews into a hastily formed ghetto, Franca somehow managed to escape Lodz and made her way to her remaining family in Warsaw.

A ghetto had been established there too, but at least, at that time, it was still possible to live as a family unit. However, father, mother and youngest daughter were already suffering as the conditions under which they were now forced to live deteriorated rapidly. Aunt Bertha decided that something had to be done to establish life outside the ghetto, particularly as the family name of Dukarevitch was non-Jewish.

Due to my uncle's good financial standing, with effective contacts among non-Jewish business friends, they eventually were able to move to lodgings in the city and even got young daughter Basia into a convent. There she was given what turned out to be temporary asylum – but not before tragedy struck. Just before the move out was accomplished, a selection was started in the ghetto. Aunt Bertha's husband was in the street rushing to return home to the beleaguered family – a situation that cost his life.

People were being driven out of their cramped quarters and into the street by German soldiers and assistant Polish police. While the beating and shooting was going on, my uncle saw a child being held by the legs and thrown out of an open second floor window. Seeing that was just too much for him because, according to other witnesses, he collapsed on the pavement and died – apparently from a heart attack.

Now only my aunt and two cousins remained. As they all had the looks and language of typical Poles, they hastened their escape from the further horrors of ghetto life and managed to find lodgings in a nearby suburb that had not yet suffered the ravages of war. Thanks again to faithful Polish friends and remaining savings they even managed to get official non-Jewish identity documents, so necessary before they could leave the ghetto.

With great difficulty and great personal trauma, they managed to retrieve Basia from the friendly convent (the trauma was largely caused by the unwilling child herself). It seems that due to the kindness of the mother superior and some of her nuns she had quickly responded to Catholic dogma and convent life. She even refused to acknowledge her family whom she now recognized as being foreign to her. When she was told that her family was Jewish, she screamed that she hated the Jews for killing Christ and refused to allow herself to be taken away. However, after days of strenuous persuasion and some mild arm-twisting, she reluctantly agreed to go to her new home, but for some time remained rebellious and difficult.

From that time until well after the War, as far as the neighbours were concerned they observed a 'normal' Polish family consisting of Franka, who changed her role to that of a loving mother, and her younger sister, who now became her daughter and was renamed Barbara. Aunt Bertha became a gentle, dignified, living-in nanny. As the child grew she attended a neighbouring school wearing a large cross that she often fondled. Franka and Barbara took on a new identifying surname, as did Bertha, so that no trace of being Jews remained.

Even a suspicion of Jewishness on the part of the Poles was dangerous. As the War ended, the sad, meagre remnants of the concentration camps began drifting back in the hope of finding some of their families alive. For most this was a hopeless quest aggravated by intense danger. Many Poles resented this return and turned to violence and murder to get rid of these unwanted survivors. It is known that in many cases these killings were perpetrated by those who profited by taking over or stealing Jewish owned property from those millions of Polish Jews that the Germans had sought to destroy.

The sad, now penniless Dukarevitch family eventually left Poland and settled in Paris, where they lived for many years. Franca died a frail old lady in 1999. Aunt Bertha was hit by a car as she crossed a road in 1982; but Barbara retired as a professor at the Sorbonne some years ago. She shares a home with a brilliant son who is now making his way in French life as an academic.

On my mother's return from Lodz, we sent a telegram to my two uncles in South Africa. From the beginning of the War, my mother had constantly told me to remember my uncles' post office box number there. In fact, right up until our clothes were taken from us, I always had a piece of paper with that number sewn into the hem of my dress. 'In case something happens to me and you survive,' my mother would say, 'You must know where to contact them.' We were not sure how the War had affected them because we had heard that the South Africans had fought against Germany. However, my uncles were beside themselves with joy when they eventually received our telegram. They had not expected to receive any good news. However, they became desperate because they could not acknowledge receipt of our communication.

They went from post office to post office, but no one knew where Koeslin was. I do not know how they resolved this difficulty, but eventually we received the anxiously awaited reply. These were exciting times and every few days we would receive news of other survivors. Our thoughts were beginning to turn to Latvia. We wanted to go back as soon as possible. We still had hopes of finding some members of our family alive.

One day, my mother and one of the German dressmakers were travelling to a nearby town to fit a dress that had been ordered for Ala Popova, a famous actress and beautiful wife of a general. On their return journey the jeep in which they had been travelling overturned and my mother was grievously injured and taken to hospital. As soon as I was informed, I rushed to the hospital where I was met by the same doctor who had operated on me. He shrugged his shoulders and said, 'You must not hold out much hope for your mother's survival – she is very badly injured. We shall do what we can, but she has fractured the base of her skull.' 'Oh G–d,' I prayed, 'You must save her. After all that we have been through, you can't take her away'. For the first month, the doctors held out little hope. The doctor and his wife were even preparing to adopt me should anything happen to her. The documents were all signed and I sent a telegram to my aunt in Lodz asking her to come as my mother was in a critical condition.

Aunt Bertha arrived shortly in a tearful state and settled down in our room to await events. Her presence must have helped my mother because she soon showed signs of what was to become a slow recovery.

In a short while Aunt Bertha decided she must return home.

Freedom and Flight

As she and her family were left desperately poor after the War, my mother urged her to take whatever clothes she may need from our wardrobe to help her face a cold winter. I did not see what she took. Tearful farewells followed, particularly in the hospital where my mother was to remain for some time after Bertha's departure. Slowly and painfully my mother's recovery progressed. The kind attention and especially the prepared food that had been prescribed must have contributed to her fighting spirit. When she was eventually allowed visitors, there was a constant stream of people in and out of her room. Even the general in command of the district paid his respects one rainy afternoon, causing quite a flutter in the hospital. On that occasion his opinion of my mother was further enhanced by an unexpected incident.

Standing next to my mother's bed, he noticed on her bedside table a letter addressed to her from Elya Ehrenburg, the famous Russian author and international newspaper correspondent. 'Oh!' he said, 'You correspond with Ehrenburg?' 'Not exactly,' she replied. 'This letter is from a boy, Sioma Spungin, a distant relative of ours, who was the only survivor of the Spungin family.' When the Jews were evacuated from Latvia, this boy somehow managed to escape and hid himself in some village. When the Russian Armies were advancing and came into this village, he ran out of his hiding place and ran up to the first officer he came across. This officer turned out to be Elya Ehrenburg. Sioma, who must then have been 14 or 15, told him of his background and remembered that he had an aunt living in Leningrad, but did not know her name. Elya Ehrenburg took pity on him and made an appeal on the Leningrad Radio for her to come forward, which she did. However, for many years afterwards, Sioma was under Ehrenburg's care.

This was the first letter mother had received from him when he discovered that we were alive. Ehrenburg added a few words to make himself known to my mother, and also confirmed the story. Sioma Spungin, now retired, lives in Israel and was a well-known Tass journalist during his working years.

Within a month or so, whilst my mother was still hospitalized, I received a telegram from my aunt inviting me to Lodz. My mother agreed that I should go, so I packed my little suitcase and headed for the station. Because the trains were still running irregularly, I had to wait at the station for nearly a day until the stationmaster called out, 'Train to Lodz'. I boarded it – a cattle truck – and sat throughout the journey on my uncomfortable suitcase. Although I was 16, it was my first outing into the world on my own and I was bewildered. On arrival, I stopped someone to ask for directions and received very long and complicated instructions. Lodz was a big city and I had to take a tram, get off at such and such a stop and then cross the road and catch another tram that would take me to my destination. When I got off the tram, I saw a long queue waiting for the next bus. As I was nervously crossing the road to join the seemingly endless crowd, something familiar caught my eye. It was a blouse just like my mother's, but was being worn by a strange woman. I went up to her and asked if she was Franca Chwat. She smiled with surprise and said, 'Yes'. 'I am your cousin Maja,' I replied. It was my mother's blouse that my aunt had taken when she visited us and had obviously passed on to her daughter. It later transpired that they had summoned me for no particular reason other than that they felt I needed a break from the pressures of my mother's illness. I spent a week with them and returned to Koeslin.

On one occasion Dina and I were paying a visit to a dental clinic situated in a large cavernous room full of Russian soldiers. As was to be expected, the soldiers were making good-natured passes, but we just ignored them. However, the soldier sitting next to us kept on muttering and every time we stopped talking he would look at us and say something. We suddenly realized he was not speaking Russian, and it dawned on us that he was mumbling a password used amongst the survivors to establish whether you were Jewish. The word was *Amcho*, meaning 'Of Your People'. Once we realized what he was saying, we were happy to make his acquaintance and discovered that he was from Ponevesh, my mother's birthplace. We invited him to visit us at home. There we heard his story and animated reminiscences followed. It turned out that he knew some of our family who were living there before the War. He told us that one of my cousins, Polia,

Freedom and Flight

and her father had survived after escaping to Russia early in the War. They had spent the war years in Tashkent, a remote city in the hinterland, and had now returned to Vilna after a long return journey.

I could not believe what I heard, for we had not held out much hope of their being alive. This soldier, Aba Katzen, visited us constantly thereafter. He, too, was the only survivor of a large family. He also told us how poverty-stricken the people returning to their birthplace were. He had visited Latvia and Lithuania and talked to the survivors. His impression of the area was that we had no reason to hurry back, although until then, all our thoughts had been directed towards going home. We had even progressed to the point where we had been sent to a special investigation camp run by the Russian Secret Police to establish our identity and were given clearance to return.

The more we saw of Aba, the more we doubted the wisdom of returning, particularly as news reached us of survivors who had returned and had been murdered by the local population in Lithuania and Poland. Not only was vicious racial intolerance the main cause but it transpired that many neighbours in these areas of Jewish annihilation had moved into the victims' houses after looting the household belongings. Had the survivors returned to their homes, a clash would have occurred that murder would clearly resolve; hence the continuing bestiality of some Poles and Lithuanians.

We were eventually persuaded to turn westwards instead. For us this appeared easier and less risky to accomplish, particularly because of my mother's brothers in South Africa. Furthermore, the West did not look as hostile to us as it did to other women who were now confused and lost. Many evenings were now spent by all of us trying to remember some distant relative in America, Palestine or Africa. But these exercises proved fruitless, as even when a name was recalled, addresses were unknown.

Fred, one of our Polish friends, who used to travel quite often to Lodz and other Polish towns, came back from one of his trips with news that changed all of our lives. In Liegnitz, he said, there was a big Jewish organization called the Brecha, which was helping all the Jews who wanted to go to Palestine.

This opened a whole new vista for us, including our Russian soldier, Aba. Fred became our secret agent. He would travel back and forth making all sorts of clandestine arrangements for us, because by now we were Russian citizens attached to the Russian Army and departure to the West would be rated as desertion.

Russian agents were all over East Germany and mother was well known as a personal friend of high-ranking officers' families. The women of our group, one by one, took a trip to Lignitz under all sorts of pretexts, mostly 'to look for surviving relatives'. We were all preparing to escape and go our separate ways. Quietly, and without arousing much suspicion, we started selling off our acquisitions. The most sought-after items were the private sewing machines and the baby grand pianos. Even my pet dog, Muska, was given away to a kind German lady who worked in our sewing workshop. To this day, I remember my tears as Muska disappeared in a large open-topped sewing bag.

While Ginda was away making arrangements, Dina heard of a German woman who wanted to buy her piano. She sold it to her, received the cash and was very happy with the deal. Ginda returned and nearly fainted when Dina told her that she had sold the piano. Unbeknown to Dina, Ginda had hidden in the piano all their most precious possessions, such as small bits of jewellery that they had saved all through the camps by concealing them internally and managing to avoid gynaecological inspections. Now they were all gone. The woman who had bought the piano proved to be untraceable.

Events moved rapidly. The Russians decided to move out of East Prussia and our factory was to be handed over to the East Germans. Officially, we were now preparing to return to our beloved homeland, but with Fred's help secret arrangements of a different kind were now finalized.

A year had elapsed since our arrival in Koeslin and now, on an early summer day, mother and I simply walked out of our comfortable home, without any goodbyes, never to return. We headed for the station each with a small bag in hand and enough money in our wallets to purchase train tickets to Lignitz. Though a year had elapsed since the War had ended, most of the travellers were soldiers in a variety of uniforms. A

Freedom and Flight

more relaxed atmosphere prevailed and civilian faces generally were rounder and happier than during those terrifying days of a year ago.

There were no more frightening identity checks and after an uneventful journey we arrived at our destination. Enquiries led us directly to the offices we sought where our prepared papers were awaiting us. To frustrate any Russian enquiries our real names were dropped and we officially became Shatz – my mother's maiden name.

We were now under the care of the Brecha. This organization comprised a brave band of young Jews who were sent from Palestine to facilitate the movement of Jewish survivors of the Holocaust who wished to settle there. This operation had to be carried out clandestinely, as Palestine was still part of the British Empire and was administered from Whitehall under the British mandate. Official immigration was limited by law to a trickle, and the tragedies and acts of heroism to which this infamous state of affairs gave rise, are now part of history.

Immediately after receipt of the papers, we were directed back to the railway station where a train with Germans being repatriated back to Germany was to leave soon. At this time the 'Polish Corridor', as this area was called, was being cleared of Germans who settled there mainly after the German occupation of Poland. Trainloads of these people were leaving weekly and the Brecha had arranged that a few coaches of each transport would be allocated to Jewish refugees being passed off as German nationals.

As our immediate destination was Vienna, we were being routed through Czechoslovakia. Border guards were persuaded to let the Jewish refugees through, on condition that the Brecha ensured that everybody falling under this arrangement was, in fact, Jewish. At one of the checkpoints, where the Brecha members were making sure that only Jews were passing, people would be asked to identify themselves by saying something typically Jewish. I was stopped. 'Are you Jewish?', was the question. 'What a question!' I replied in Hebrew. They smiled and let me go.

As the train wound through Czechoslovakia, it would frequently stop to give the passengers a chance to get out and buy food. At one such stop, my mother went to look for some friends by the name of Feinberg who were on the same train a few coaches away from us. As she was walking along the track, she heard a voice calling 'Madam Zarch, Madam Zarch', and a woman came running after her. What a surprise! This woman was the daughter of neighbours of ours in Dvinsk. I vividly remember the hefty and friendly woman who, on seeing me, would always give me a big squeeze and a hug, while my face was pressed against her big soft bosom, which more often that not smelt of *gefilte* fish or some other kitchen odour. Her daughter Lea was a music student in Riga and had married the son of a very well-known family by the name of Apter. During the German onslaught, part of the family managed to escape to Russia. There they spent all the war years. After the War, they devised a plan to escape to the West instead of returning to Riga. In their case it was not very easy, but because they were people of means, they managed to persuade a pilot to fly their whole family into Poland. From there, with the help of the Brecha, they too were now escaping on this train. We were overjoyed to meet them. They were a big family, and Mr Apter knew exactly what he wanted to do and how to go about it. They invited my mother and me to join them and we continued the journey together. This meeting had an interesting sequel in Paris later.

On arrival in Vienna, we were met by two very young-looking Brecha members who shepherded us into covered vans and transported us to barrack-like buildings in the city. The next day, the same vans drove us to the main transit camp in Austria situated in the fairy-tale city of Salzburg.

This camp, which was to be our home for nearly six weeks, was under American Army jurisdiction and was efficiently organized. It was opposite the beautiful Franz Joseph Church and had a lovely view of the surrounding mountains. Nearly every day people arrived with very little hope of speedily moving on to Palestine – their final destination. Britain was using every possible means, foul or fair, to throttle off the immigrant stream to a mere trickle, so those who had barely survived the inhumanity of the Holocaust were now to languish again, but this time in Displaced Persons (DP) camps for the homeless or in the Mediterranean on board rusting

Freedom and Flight

immigrant ships with nowhere to go. Once again but in much smaller numbers, many died throughout Europe because of newly acquired diseases or tragically at sea or on land, due to British efforts to forcibly prevent settlement in Palestine.

The hunt for relatives in other parts of the world was intensified. The Apters had a relation in America and decided to direct their efforts at being allowed to go there. We wanted to go to South Africa to join my uncles, but visas were not available and the wait would be very long. For the time being, we thought Palestine would be a good stepping-stone. Mother knew many people there, although none of them were relatives.

Life in the Salzburg DP camp was crowded and unpleasant. However, the city and its surroundings compensated for all these shortcomings. By obtaining a permit from the office, we were able to wander around this beautiful city and visit the castle on the hill. Luckily we still had some money from our sale in Koeslin so were not short of essentials. We would go to the Marionette Theatre a few times during the week, and we heard Yehudi Menuhin play in Salzburg during that summer. The young Apters used to make excursions into the country and occasionally we would join them. Exploring the hills and valleys of Austria was a great joy, but the people were suspicious and unfriendly. Then, one day, something completely unexpected happened to change our course of direction.

The famous American, Rabbi Hillel Silver, was visiting the DP camps. Mr Apter knew Rabbi Silver personally and decided to call on him. During this visit, it was discovered that Rabbi Silver was in possession of Venezuelan visas and was empowered to issue these to prospective Jewish immigrants as a token of that country's humanity. The route was to be through Paris. Mr Apter returned triumphantly with visas for his whole family, but not for us. Our friends, the Feinbergs, also wanted to reach America, and when they heard of the Apter's luck, Mr Feinberg decided to seek a meeting with Rabbi Silver. 'Perhaps he will do the same for us even if I don't know him personally,' he said to my mother, hopefully. After an interminable wait, he returned in triumph waving the necessary visas.

To Forgive... But Not Forget

With the Apters and Feinbergs leaving, we felt forgotten and forlorn. My mother decided to wire my uncles for advice, but no immediate answer was forthcoming. In the meantime, our Brecha organizers were forming another group of immigrant hopefuls for an assault on the guarded Palestine coast. We were listed for the next ship sailing soon from a secret port.

The day before we were supposed to leave, we received a reply from my uncles: 'Proceed to Paris. Money waiting at the Paris Joint Distribution Committee.' We were overjoyed; our problem was resolved. Now we could again join the Apters and go with them to Paris.

One evening, a friendly young American soldier who worked in the camp office, invited me to the cinema. During the course of conversation, I told him that we were planning to go to Paris. He told me that he had recently returned from that most beautiful city and, in fact, had two francs in his pocket that he gave to me. As we walked out of the camp gate and turned the corner, I heard someone calling me. I turned round and saw Ginda. What a surprise that was! We were overjoyed to see each other, for since their escape we had lost contact with them. She told me that her sister, Dina, had married a man from Vilna, and they were all in another DP camp not far from Salzburg. I was so excited that I excused myself from going to the cinema and rushed back to the camp with Ginda. She told us how Dina had met and married her husband, but that they had no money to buy rings. The next day mother took them to town and bought wedding rings for them and we arranged a little party. I visited them in camp several times and had to share a bed with Dina and her husband because there was nowhere else to sleep.

The date was set for our departure for Paris. We bought third-class train tickets and boarded a train full of Arab soldiers. They were very correct and made room for us in the crowded carriage. Nadia, the Apter's eight-year-old daughter, was put to sleep on a bench and we were all set for the night. Suddenly, we were awakened by Leah Apter who was panic-stricken. She could not find Nadia, so all of us ran about looking for her. An Arab, who had also been awakened by the commotion, realized what was happening even though we spoke Russian. He lifted his greatcoat from the seat and

Freedom and Flight

revealed, to our relief, the peacefully sleeping Nadia. He told us in halting German that she had looked so cold he had decided to take off his coat and cover her. After the hate and horror of war this small incident led us to believe that human kindness was not yet quite dead.

We arrived in Paris the next morning. We looked around the big station feeling very lost and helpless. We had no French money and did not know where to change what we had left of our German currency. Suddenly, I remembered the two French francs given to me by my soldier friend that, in those days, was the price of a Metro ticket.

Mr Apter, who vaguely knew Paris, was sent to investigate. After a long, anxious wait, he arrived towards evening with a huge, blond-haired man who was the representative of the Joint Distribution Committee. We had spent the whole day on the station without food or water and felt extremely miserable by then. We were taken to a Jewish organization by taxi where we were fed, given food coupons and money and allocated to the Hotel de Cadix, not far from the Versailles Metro station. We, with Mr Feinberg and his mother, spent the next few weeks there.

For the first time in months we slept in a clean bed with sheets, had a hot bath and felt human again. Our only regret was that the Apters were not with us; they were accommodated in a boarding house run by a Jewish religious organization, which was far from our quarters.

The following morning we set out to find a post office to send a telegram to my uncles in South Africa and then went in quest of the Joint Distribution Committee offices to receive the money awaiting our arrival. We felt on top of the world when we discovered that we had been sent £200. For the first few days, life in Paris was hard but exciting. We knew no French and this presented us with great problems, but we soon overcame them by acquiring a few key phrases like, 'Where is the Metro?' However, knowing Yiddish was a great help because, no matter from which part of the world they came, the older generation of Jews had this language in common.

We started regular correspondence with my uncles and most of their letters contained £10 or £20. Thanks to them, we were short of nothing. We even received a parcel of clothing that was most useful, but it broke my heart when a pair of black, patent-leather shoes were just too small. We learnt from their letters that Uncle Dave had married and both he and Uncle Leon were in the hotel business. One day, we received a letter from Uncle Dave's new wife, Lola. Before the War, she had an aunt and cousin living in Dvinsk. Did we by any chance know them or what had happened to them? Their name was Gutstein. Mrs Gutstein's daughter was Leah Apter, the woman who had recognized my mother on the platform in Czechoslovakia during our flight from Poland and had become our friend and travelling companion ever since! We rushed over to her hotel to show her the letter. She burst out crying, not believing such a coincidence. From then on they corresponded, and a year or so later Leah visited her aunt in South Africa.

My Uncle Leon's letters were always full of ideas. What we should do; what we should buy. He also gave us addresses of people in Paris. The first address we investigated belonged to a couple by the name of Khelmer. Mr Khelmer was an old school friend of a Mr Abramovitch, a friend of both my uncles. Mr Abramovitch and his wife came from Rostov-on-Don in Russia. Although they now lived in different countries, they still corresponded. On hearing from my uncle of our plight in Paris, Mr Abramovitch insisted on my uncle sending us the Khelmers' address. He himself wrote direct to his friend, telling him what he knew about us and asking him to do all he could for us. When we knocked on their door we were met with outstretched arms as if we were long-lost friends. In fact, they said, they had already known about us and had a parcel of clothing waiting for us, as they had obviously expected to see beggars in rags.

We eventually became great friends and during the course of our visits to them, Mr Khelmer would relate to us all the news he had received from his friend in South Africa. His friend, he told us, had a gifted son completing his architectural studies and the thought had crossed his mind that it would be nice if, when we got to South Africa, he took a liking to me. This idea was dispelled by my mother who said that I had had no youth and had a lot to catch up with; at the age of 17, I had a long way to go before marriage.

Freedom and Flight

Another address was that of Mr and Mrs Sherman. My mother had vague recollections of a handsome young man named Srolik Sherman who had left Ponevesh in Lithuania in the 1920s. When we traced him we arranged to call on him the next day. When a bald Mr Sherman opened the door, after a few minutes silence she said, 'Oh Srolik, how you've changed!' – a compliment I am sure he did not appreciate! She had forgotten the span of 20 years. They became close friends and rendered us immeasurable assistance right through our stay in Paris. Until Mr Sherman's death a few years ago, we remained in close contact.

Because of the warmth of the Shermans' friendship we decided to find a hotel closer to them. In any case, the regular financial support from my uncles enabled us to live more comfortably. We gave up our cramped attic room at the Hotel de Cadix, and moved to a larger room in a more expensive hotel at 51 Rue Louriston round the corner from the Shermans. They had a beautiful second floor flat in a very fashionable building just off the Arc de Triomphe. Mr Sherman had established a very exclusive tailoring establishment after they settled in Paris during the early 1930s, and most of his patrons were from the elite of the international diplomatic corps.

During the year we lived in Paris, awaiting our papers to emigrate to South Africa we met many refugees. Some were from our hometown and others we knew from our various concentration camps. Dora Rein was one of them. She was a lovely blonde girl of about 18 who came from Dvinsk, and was with us in the ghetto where she lost all her family. Later, she moved to the Citadel and then to Kaiserwald where I lost track of her. We were overjoyed to see each other, but years later we were to meet again in different circumstances. We also, to our delight, met Shienale Ichlov. It was she who had been sent away ill from Sophienwald and had been given up for dead.

More survivors were arriving in Paris and we experienced some dramatic reunions. One day there was a knock on our door, which was opened by my mother. There, haggard and sad, stood the woman from Vilna who, in the Gottendorf camp, had given my mother some of the potato peels she had recovered from the toilet. She had heard that we had survived and were in Paris and had managed to track us down to 'claim the cake', as she put it, that my mother had promised her in return for those miserable potato peels. Many tears of sorrow and joy were shed together as we reminisced late into the night. Needless to say, we had cake for supper.

Another chance meeting was with a lovely blonde girl who had lived near our home in Dvinsk. She was a year older than me, but had regained her beauty after liberation. Her entire family perished in the Holocaust and she was embarking on a lonely odyssey looking for friends who might have survived. I had last seen her in Kaiserwald and was sure she was dead. Unbeknown to us we were shortly to meet again in South Africa.

We met many new and interesting people at the Shermans, but continued to be involved in refugee circles that were fast developing in Paris at that time. The French Government was wonderful towards the refugees in the years after the War. They gave all the assistance they could. Most of the refugees came without any papers of identification whatsoever.

The French Prefecture and Police worked overtime to issue everyone with documents. During the course of issuing our papers, a group of us were taken to the Isle de Cité to have our fingerprints taken and various forms completed. After being detained for most of the day in a big cell-like room, we were called out to go to another office. As we were walking along a corridor we looked into the courtyard below and, to our astonishment, saw German soldiers and officers running around and shouting in German, with guns and tanks standing nearby. We stood transfixed. Our relief – when we were told that it was a film that was being made – was indescribable. After we received our identity cards, we were issued with ration cards that were exactly the same as that of any Frenchman, a pair of shoes every birthday, materials – so many yards per person – and various other things.

The sympathy and friendliness of the Parisians restored my faith in people and I grew to love Paris. I learnt French and became completely fluent, to the extent that people often did not believe that I was a foreign refugee. My hair grew thick again after my bout of typhus on liberation nearly two years earlier, and its golden colour set off my blue eyes, with a returned lustre that somehow belied my recent history. Visiting art galleries and going to concerts and operas became part of a very active social life. The ancient streets of Paris never ceased to charm me and my developing interest in architecture must have been a premonition of a rather different future.

My mother's cultural guidance – as part of her decision to intensively further my lost years of education – was the key to my developing love of Paris and of things beautiful. Little could I even imagine that my future life in a warm and friendly country would be so enriched by my French experiences.

At last, we heard the good news that our visas for South Africa were about to be granted. It had taken my uncles almost a year to obtain permission for us to enter South Africa. All the negotiations were done through the Joint Distribution Committee. During one of her visits to that office, mother noticed a lovely, dark, lady working at a desk. She turned to me and said, 'You know that woman has a very familiar face.' She went up to her and her hunch was confirmed; it was a school friend of hers whom she had not seen for 30 years. There, I also met a girl by the name of Henia Abramowitz. Although I had not known it at the time, she had also been in Kaiserwald and had originally come from Vilna where she lost her whole family. She had been waiting many months to join her only relative, an aunt in South Africa. Eventually, when we came to South Africa, our lives ran almost parallel. We married within a year of each other, lived in the same block of flats and, by coincidence, we later built our houses round the corner from each other. Our boys attended the same nursery school, were both at the University of the Witwatersrand and are firm friends.

In August 1947 we left Paris via London for South Africa. In London we stayed for a week with an old schoolfriend my mother had discovered through friends in Paris. We then embarked at Southampton on the *Durban Castle* for South Africa with hopes for a new life and a brighter future.

South Africa

Recalling our horrific voyages on the Baltic nearly three years before, the *Durban Castle* was an inkling of heaven. The sea was a calm, deep green-blue and the food was certainly six-star. Two weeks on board this gracious ship gave us a chance to have a much-needed rest, to reflect on our past and to speculate on the future. We met some very nice people returning to South Africa from a trip abroad. I particularly recollect one lady from Cape Town who told us much about life in South Africa. Also on board was a Mrs Diesenhaus, who had come from Paris with us and was going to South Africa to remarry.

A day of two before we were due to dock, I suddenly remembered that there were people I knew in South Africa: the Treger family who had left Dvinsk for South Africa in 1938. At Cape Town docks we were met by my Uncle Leon, who had come from Johannesburg to welcome us to our new land. During our stay in Cape Town, uncle showed us the town. He was generous, charitable, and happy to have us alive with him.

During our few days sojourn in 'The Mother City', as Cape Town is known, we were shown the sights of this glorious and gregarious metropolis. Nothing in Europe had prepared us for this wonderful cocktail of friendliness, warm sunlight, blue skies and the magnificent backdrop of towering Table Mountain. What was especially surprising was how well the generally smiling, rich racial mix of people in the teeming streets seemed to get on with each other. Uncle Leon explained that the impression Cape Town gives on this issue was not necessarily what we would find in the more northerly cities in this extensive country.

After the few days of being enchanted by beautiful inland farms, old white gabled buildings, beautiful vistas of pine forests, twisting old streets and fine golden beaches which stretched almost as far as the eye could see, it was time to leave for our future home.

The train journey to Johannesburg was spent in relating our experiences and, unfortunately, dispelling any hopes that uncle might have had that more family members had survived. He already knew about the survival of my cousins from Daugavpils as they had also contacted him.

At the Johannesburg station a big reception committee was awaiting us – my other uncle and his wife, Mr and Mrs Abramovitch and several others. From the station we were taken to Uncle Dave's house, where we spent the night repeating the story of our experiences. They had a beautiful home set in a magnificent garden in a hilltop suburb called Mountainview. This was the first time in nearly seven years that we had lived in normal conditions in a house and it was paradise to us. The next day, Sunday, I was told that I would be taken for a drive by Mr Abramovitch's son, Sidney. I was later told that this fellow had agreed under protest to show 'the foreign girl' something of Johannesburg, so when I got to the car I found his sister Monica there. He was taking her along to keep him company in case he could not talk to me. As it turned out, they both spoke Russian and we spent a rather pleasant morning – much to his surprise.

The next few days proved to be a blur of people and faces. Uncle Dave and wife Lola were well known for their hospitality and had many friends. All of these seemed to want to meet us. At the core of these visits was curiosity, a need to establish if any relatives in Europe that we may have known had survived and just plain warm friendliness.

After spending a few days with Uncle Dave, Lola and their baby son Boris, we left for a neighbouring industrial town called Germiston where Uncle Leon owned a large hotel. Here some of Leon's more impatient friends came calling immediately, hoping to hear news of Latvian relatives. However, the following Sunday he organized a huge reception in our honour so that all his friends could meet us. Over 300 people crowded his banqueting hall. It was a moving, but at the same time a rather sad occasion. Many people who had come in the hope of hearing good news about their relatives left with heavy hearts after hearing our story.

I am happy, though, to say that at least one person, who least expected to receive any news, had a pleasant surprise. Mother heard that one of her schoolfriends was living nearby and telephoned him. He was not at home and his wife answered the telephone. Mother explained her reason for telephoning and during the conversation asked his wife where she came from. 'Oh, you would not know me,' she said, 'I come from Riga, Latvia, and heard that all my family except one sister who left for Russia when I was a little girl, was killed.' 'What is your maiden name?', mother asked. She told her. 'Tell me,' mother said, 'was your sister's name so and so?' 'Why yes, did you know her?' 'Not only do I know her, but just over a year ago I met her and her husband, both doctors, and we became great friends. I have her address.' The woman on the other end of the line was speechless! Within 15 minutes she was with us, with a whole pile of photographs for my mother to confirm that it really was her sister. This new-found sister was the woman major that had become such a close friend in Koeslin!

Meanwhile, uncle prepared a beautiful but small flat for us in Johannesburg. Mrs Stiller, who had travelled on the boat from Paris with us as Mrs Diesenhaus, also managed to get a flat in the same building. Life became a whirl. I soon made many friends and saw a lot of Sidney Abramovitch. One particular friend was a girl by the name of Ghita Joffe. For her twenty-first birthday she was to have a large party to which she invited Sidney and me. A day or so before the party I saw Mrs Stiller, who told me that her son, Oles, would be arriving from Paris to visit her and asked me whether I would entertain him and introduce him to young people during his stay. I thought the party would provide a good opportunity and asked Ghita if she would mind my bringing him. Oles was an immediate success with the hostess and they danced together for most of the evening. About midnight, he came to me and told me that he had found a cousin there. I didn't believe him and thought he was either pulling my leg or drunk, but he insisted that it was so. The following morning his mother confirmed that this was indeed a second cousin. She had been evacuated from Poland with a group of children during the War and the family had not known what had happened to her. To add to this coincidence, Oles married Ghita soon afterwards.

The flat in Johannesburg was now complete and we moved in. Remembering that my mother had studied music in Berlin's music conservatory, my uncle bought me a beautiful Blüthner baby grand piano, which he had placed in our new lounge. To everybody's admiration all the furniture in the flat was stinkwood. I hated it and many a night cried because of its gloomy effect. I would have liked light furniture, the dark museum pieces in such a small flat reminded me of the darkness of the past. I was often angry with myself for not being thankful for I later realized the value of that stinkwood furniture.

Generally speaking both my uncles were very kind to us. Uncle Leon supported us from the day of our arrival in South Africa. I had everything I ever wanted. He enjoyed my company and would take me on all his shopping trips. One of those trips was especially important. Having entered a second-hand furniture shop belonging to a Mr Rein, he, as always, would introduce me, telling the story of how I, his niece, had been saved from the Holocaust.

Hearing the story in great sympathy, Mr Rein, with sadness on his face, told me that all his relatives were killed. Remembering the girl by the name of Rein who was with us as a survivor, I asked where he came from. He said Latvia. I asked him to tell me if he perhaps knew of any relative by the name of Dora Rein. The man nearly fainted. 'That is my niece,' he said. I told him the whole story. Her parents were killed and she obviously did not know where to find him. I managed to trace her in Paris and put them in touch. A few months later, while on holiday at the Cape, I met Dora at the docks in Cape Town and introduced her to her tearful uncle who naturally had come from Johannesburg to meet her.

I enrolled at Damelin, a private college, to take my 'matric', but before that I was to spend the summer holidays in Muizenberg – a well-known holiday resort in the Cape, especially popular with the older South African Jewish community. I was looking forward to this very much, for by then I had found out that the Treger family, my special friends from Dvinsk, were living in Cape Town.

On the train I was keenly anticipating the outcome of our meeting. Would I recognize my playmate from so long ago? What if she did not remember me? It was over ten years since we had sadly parted when we were only little girls. I telephoned her as soon as we arrived in Muizenberg. It was a Saturday evening and Chaya's elder sister, Riva, answered. In my rather halting English I asked to speak to Chaya. She immediately realized I was a foreigner, as Chaya's name had been changed to Anne soon after they had come to South Africa. It was not difficult for me to identify myself. Riva remembered me very well and was very excited to hear from me. I gave her a brief outline of our past experiences and the sad news that her aunt had been killed. We arranged for Chaya to telephone me the following morning. At the crack of dawn the telephone rang and we agreed to meet at the steps of the Balmoral Hotel in Muizenberg. She recognized me immediately – by my teeth – she said, because I had a gap between my front teeth. She had become a lovely young lady whom I would not have recognized had I met her in the street. There was so much to catch up on, but what was absolutely incredible was the way in which she had guessed that I had telephoned the previous night. She had returned home late and found, to her surprise, all the lights on and her father, mother and sister all sitting round the table looking very sad. As soon as she came in her sister asked in great excitement, 'Who do you think phoned?' 'Maja,' Anne replied without any hesitation. To this day, she cannot explain what made her say it. She had known nothing of my whereabouts since our parting at the dacha in 1938. Once more, one of those inexplicable things!

After my return to Johannesburg, we corresponded regularly. In one of her letters she wrote that she had met a young architect and fallen in love with him whilst on holiday in Port Elizabeth. He turned out to be the son of our house doctor. They were married soon afterwards. She became a singer of repute, which was not surprising as she had excelled herself at singing lessons in school. Her talent and beautiful voice matured as she reached adulthood and eventually became a respected teacher of singing.

The predictions of our friend in Paris came true. Some years later I married Sidney Abramovitch, who by then had become a noted architect. Twenty-five years after our Muizenberg meeting, Anne's talented husband, Mannie Feldman, joined my husband's architectural firm as a partner in the Johannesburg office.

I have now experienced over four decades of tranquil married life with two daughters and two sons. Both daughters and a son are now married to wonderful spouses. On 9 June 1976, I became a grandmother and now have seven lovely grandchildren. I am deeply grateful that my mother had been spared to share much of this happiness as a lively and proud great-grandmother.

She passed on in 1993, aged 98. Till the very end she was a lively and wise matriarch who developed a wide circle of adoring friends throughout South Africa. We shall all miss her to the end of our days.

This completes the saga of that portion of my life which, because of its tragic message, warranted this memorial – a memorial which also honours those sacred phantoms who were once real but are no more. As long as I live, they live – and perhaps even further, through my children, grandchildren, and the generations yet to follow – into – G–d's eternity.

An Ultimate Pilgrimage

For most of my life in South Africa, which now spans a period of nearly 50 years I used to dream of returning to the city of my birth: of reliving my wonderful childhood; of walking through the corridors of my school again; of spending time with my friends evoking all our joint memories; of awakening to a soft Latvian spring day and to the happiness of just being alive.

But then there were many occasions during the crisp, starry highveld nights of Johannesburg when horrible nightmares would develop to torment me. Not only would my mother and I be involved, but I would be fighting for the lives of my children. I would wake up with my body stiff with terror. And in spite of attempts at rational thinking, these dreams would thereafter haunt me for days.

However, in spite of these spells of terror, my longing to go back to visit the scenes of my childhood eventually prevailed. I also knew that it was necessary for me to pay homage at the mass graves of my dear ones and to the thousands of other victims who lay buried mainly in the dark brooding forests of Latvia.

After making this decision, I managed to trace an old school-friend Mulia Slov who, I discovered through Sioma Spungin in Riga, had been living in St Petersburg for the last 45 years. When I reached him by phone, I heard a very hesitant male voice, almost as if the owner was reluctant to identify himself to a stranger. Imagine his flood of joy when I at last identified myself sufficiently for his memory to connect. After the many years since we last saw each other in junior school back in the late 1930s, he was suddenly confronted by someone from that distant past – someone he had taken for dead! And the prospective visitor would be arriving soon with two lovely daughters to whom she would be introducing the land and people of her distant childhood.

An Ultimage Pilgrimage

The journey started on a sunny Johannesburg afternoon, in early July of 1992. My older daughter, Diana, was my travelling companion. We were flying to London to pick up my other daughter, Karen, who had emigrated to England with her husband and two baby daughters.

As we took off in heavy cloud from Heathrow the next day, I felt totally disconnected from my known world. My doubts took over. Was I not looking for answers to enigmas, which could never be found? Was I right bringing my daughters to a country where moral depravity and cruel death had been the dominant themes?

Before I could even decide these questions, we were landing at St Petersburg's most unimpressive airport. My heart was pounding. Would I really be able to recognize a person I last saw as a child, 56 years ago? A sea of expectant searching faces greeted me in the arrivals hall. I was totally bewildered. Suddenly, smiling eyes and two outstretched arms drifted into focus. It was Mulia. He recognized us by a process of elimination – a woman of about his age attended by two smiling daughters.

With a constant babble of questions and answers and some sad but short silences, we were taxied to a large hotel. By Russian standards of the day, this place was very comfortable, but none of these issues was really material.

From this moment until we left for Riga four days later, we were living as tourists and researchers seeking a desperately sad past.

On the way to the hotel we noticed that for a city rated as the second most important in Russia, St Petersburg was amazingly empty. Street after street was almost devoid of movement even though this was a weekend. On Monday morning the mystery was resolved. We learnt that in summer months the great part of the city's inhabitants move *en masse* to their dachas in the countryside and on Monday the city is repopulated.

From the moment Mulia settled us into the hotel he was never long away from us. His knowledge of the city was awesome. In 1992 the Russians were still able to easily spot tourists and take all sorts of advantage of their ignorance with regard to local customs. Taxis, restaurants and the few shops there were, fleeced them. Mulia spoke for us in every situation and we were well protected. In spite of a pervading sadness, some situations turned out to be hilarious.

Taxi drivers were notorious for overcharging tourists – in some cases by over four times the normal fare. On the occasions that we decided to use a taxi, Mulia would step off the pavement, hail an available vehicle and arrange a fare, telling the driver that he was accompanied by relatives from the provinces to whom he was showing the city. We would then climb in. I would be seated in front with the driver and he and the girls would occupy the back. Mulia had previously warned my daughters not to say a word. As we drove off he would start a conversation with me and it would be as follows, 'How is Aunty Rosa? How is the family? Are the children married?' He would continue in this vein until we reached our destination. He tried to avoid the possibility of the driver having to address my daughters. In Russia it is not uncommon for a taxi driver to want to know the entire life history of his passengers or to attempt discussing in the greatest detail the political situation now developing in Russia.

Another hilarious situation unfolded when we were to see a performance of the ballet *Giselle* at the famous Marinsky Theatre. We were unable to find a taxi. We noticed some large tourist buses waiting for tourist groups in front of the hotel. Without any further delay Mulia started to climb into one of the buses and, with arms gesticulating, vigorously engaged the driver in intense conversation. He then summoned us to join him. On climbing in he informed us that the driver had kindly agreed to take us to the performance – for a fee. We naturally agreed and without further ado this huge vehicle lurched into gear and with four passengers on board proceeded to the Marinsky!

In spite of these complications we managed to see much of St Petersburg, a most beautiful and historic city. The brooding spirit of its founder, Peter the Great, intruded into my consciousness even as I gazed in wonder at its surviving magnificence. The stark tragedy, the deaths and near-total destruction that marked its successful resistance to capture by the Germans in the Second World War added a constant patina of sadness to our thoughts.

In spite of this we found the city to be an intellectually exhilarating place. The great theatres, parks, museums and possibly the greatest art gallery in the world, brought experiences difficult to match anywhere else. Perhaps Paris could qualify as a worthy alternative. For the sweep and majesty of great architecture set in a historic urban environment, I believe St Petersburg is unique. Even Venice does not quite compare in spite of the unmatched marine setting and glorious architecture. It is strange how experiencing the phenomenon of the 'white nights' over this great city added to the feeling of being somewhere where the dominance of spirit tends to prevail over material existence. Even the throngs of people in the streets, enjoying the strange brightness well after midnight, somehow seemed transfixed with a degree of the supernatural. All too soon our planned four-day sojourn was over. We joined the night express for the train journey to our final destination, Riga, and Daugavpils in Latvia.

Once again, we were accompanied by Mulia Slov, our indomitable guardian and guide. Though we had reserved and paid for our first-class sleeper compartment when we made the booking, we were charged extra for some obscure reason. We were required to pay $US100 each though Mulia as a Russian citizen only had to pay the equivalent of $US20. The joy of being a traveller in Russia certainly became tarnished at that point.

To add insult to injury, on climbing into our special coach – which it transpired had been reserved for tourist use only – we were assailed by an overpowering smell of unflushed toilets. On complaining to the ticket examiner he informed us that the toilet system was faulty and nothing could be done about it at this stage. Even our 'private guide' could not prevail to have us moved.

It was during this journey that we discovered that Mulia was the first cousin of Joe Slovo, a prominent activist in the anti-apartheid movement and our then senior cabinet minister in charge of housing back home in South Africa. Joe Slovo had been a brilliant lawyer but in the early days of the struggle against apartheid had fled the country, with his wife Ruth, when the cells of resistance were being cruelly hunted by the South African police. Later, working closely with President Mandela, he helped to structure the new South Africa.

When we eventually settled down to a most uncomfortable journey we discovered that the seats lifted and it appeared that

To Forgive... But Not Forget

chickens had been transported on the floor below. Even frequent and generous dousings of perfume failed to sweeten this odoriferous trip.

Early next day, as the train approached Riga through misty fields and dense forests, I became engrossed in nervous thoughts. How would I react to once again being in the Riga of Kaiserwald and bestiality? Would the mental anguish of 1943 be reawakened or would time in fact have proved a great healer? The arrival at the station was overwhelming. About a dozen people were waiting to meet us on the platform. Each was carrying a bunch of small flowers of the field. I recognized none of these kind people. Once again I was totally bewildered as I had been at St Petersburg airport five days earlier.

After a lengthy kissing session I was obliged to ask each welcomer who they were. Tears and more kissing and hugging followed as each emerged as a friend from long ago. They were my schoolfriends who remembered me from as far back as kindergarten. I was overcome by emotions. I could not stop the tears and I could hardly speak. My daughter Diana held on to me in apprehension as she feared I might faint.

After we all recovered we were taken to our hotel and an intense hour of essential reminiscences followed. Many of these survivors had been sent away to Siberia just before the outbreak of war and were lucky to survive. Story followed story but eventually we were left to rest and recover from the emotions of the moment.

At this point Mulia had to leave and returned to St Petersburg. He left behind three deeply indebted friends and very warm feelings.

The kaleidoscope of events that followed is still difficult to sort out but the next few days were to yield significant markers to the history of lives lost and memories retained.

Our first visit was to the Riga of the ancient past. Riga is still referred to by some as the 'Paris of the North'. There was virtually no fighting in its environs during the War, as at least half of its inhabitants at that time were of German extraction. It thus managed to survive unscathed. The old city is not very extensive but the narrow cobbled streets and the fabric of quaint ancient façades prevail to delight the tourist.

The famous beach in Jarmula is still a feature of the outer city

An Ultimage Pilgrimage

and stretches for miles, but swimming is not allowed because of pollution. The resorts that I remembered are still there but after the luxury and beauty I had become used to in South Africa, are not as glamorous as my memory would have me believe.

The time came for me to show Diana and Karen the places burned into my memory by the Germans. First we went to the area in Kaiserwald where, before the War, magnificent old villas stood. Now many of them were abandoned and derelict. The others generally needed painting. The gardens were unkempt and heavily overgrown. A pall of decay hung over the entire area. Disappointed, we moved on to where the concentration camp once stood adjacent to the railway. Now harsh modern blocks of flats covered the site. Not even a memorial plaque acknowledged the presence of the historic place to which human beings from half of Europe were brought for extermination. Some 200,000 Jews from all over Europe, in addition to the 80,000 Latvian Jews, were brought to Riga to be killed.

In silence we climbed into the car and proceeded to the place where the historical Riga ghetto and later German extension had been added to accommodate thousands of German Jews who were brought here to die. Just a collection of old, mainly wooden, buildings remained. It was from here that the inhabitants were removed for mass killings in the Forest of Rumboli, not far away. No plaques or memorials were evident here either. Could it be that death and mass murder was not considered a catastrophe to be commemorated? Or was the shame too great to bring the events to the attention of posterity? I doubt it. Those who wonder can draw their own conclusions.

Of special significance is the wonderful evening we spent with one of the schoolfriends who was amongst those who were at that emotional station meeting. Her name was Sarah Rosenberg. She and I were in ballet school together and both of us shared an adoration of our teacher, Madam Mirtzeva. She had mesmerized us into a love of ballet, which, in my case, remained a life-long passion. Towards the end of our pupilage, she even considered that we had reached a standard that qualified us to participate in a public performance. During the evening Sarah startled me by producing a folio of newspaper cuttings dealing with this event. It seems that the critics had been particularly impressed with us. What a pleasant surprise that was and what

To Forgive...But Not Forget

warm poignant memories this evoked.

These cuttings had a special significance for me because, strangely, at home in Johannesburg, I have a photograph taken during that performance. My mother had sent it to my Uncle Leon at that time and he gave it to me soon after we arrived in South Africa in 1947.

This happy evening took place in a very small but pleasant apartment. Dinner included all kinds of goodies that Sarah had remembered we so enjoyed as children. Her husband, a singer who had been a principal soloist with the renowned Riga Philharmonic Orchestra, sang for us after the meal. 'Songs of Sadness and Joy' I classified them in my catalogue of bittersweet memories.

One of the most painful and poignant events occurred on the Sunday of our visit. We were taken to a memorial gathering to commemorate the eventual clearing and establishment of what was once the Great Synagogue of Riga. It was known as the Great 'Choir' Synagogue in Gogol Street and was the pride of the community since it had been built in 1871. It was also the building that housed the Beth Din, the Rabbinic Court.

During 1941, one of the *Aktions* in Riga resulted in this synagogue being crammed full of captive men, women and children, mostly in families, and then the building was burnt to the ground. Just before the memorial meeting the site was finally cleared by excavation. The workers found sad relics – burnt artefacts, remains of clothing, watches and poignant items of children's jewellery such as little rings and bracelets.

The day was cold and rainy. The pathetic remnants of the Riga's survivors, about one hundred people in all, stood under umbrellas, weeping openly as someone addressed them in mournful tones. We stood transfixed and unbelieving. It had taken so long to sanctify and dedicate this important and tragic relic of faith and bestiality. At this moment Hitler's concept of a 'super race' seemed worse than the most odious offal of history.

Time was passing and our stay of four days was ending. Before we were to depart again for London and home, we had scheduled two days for the most difficult part of our pilgrimage, the one to Daugavpils. I did not believe I could withstand the reliving of my life's deep tragedy for longer than that.

Once again we were taken by car by a wonderful guide and

survivor. This time it was with Sioma Spungin, whose story I have related briefly in an earlier chapter. He was now retired as an honoured journalist and had insisted on being involved in this last stage of our odyssey.

The road was good and the scenery beautiful. Giant birches lined the winding road in many places as a foreground to thick forests beyond. Small farming hamlets provided the aesthetic relief. As South Africans who were used to frequent filling station complexes on our long distance express ways, we found it very strange that here exceedingly long distances were being travelled with no possibility of a refuelling stop.

Almost right through this journey we were deeply engrossed in childhood reminiscences relating to our hometown. I had the feeling that Sioma, who travelled this road often to visit friends, was preparing me for what we were about to see. The approach to Daugavpils is dramatic. A huge metal bird-like sculpture on a slow bend into the city announces the name of Daugavpils and it's founding year, 1272. Beyond are dark green trees and a vista of orange roofs. A high church steeple adds drama to the scene. Faith seems to dominate where none had existed to prevent the stark tragedy that overcame this place not so very long ago.

I had a lump in my throat. Diana and Karen stared unblinking ahead into what must have been, to them, a setting for horrors they should never ever have to experience. For me, so many memories surged through my mind. What will I now find? Whom will I meet? How will the city now look? Will I find the street where I lived? Will I be able to tell my daughters all I ever wanted to say to them about my childhood?

We were now entering my hometown and Sioma started to explain where we were. I tried hard to orientate myself and get my bearings. Half a century had passed, a long time from childhood to middle age. Much water had literally flowed under the bridges over the River Dvina, which dominates the city.

We stopped at a group of buildings in the town centre. These housed the only remaining Jewish organization of the many that existed at the beginning of the War. One of its important functions was to take care of the few elderly survivors who had returned from Siberia and the extermination camps. It became obvious to me that they were so short of funding that the poor and the sick lived at a miserable level of existence. How sad after all that they had gone through. I resolved to do something about this on my return home.

Another activity interested me. This was their looking after the huge mass graves of victims murdered in the surrounding forests and putting up monuments funded by some of the few luckier ones who were able to make a success of their shattered lives. While having coffee, we heard about the generally unhappy life the few Jews in the town had been able to establish and I enquired about my friends of long ago who may have been among them. It seemed that my generation had been effectively wiped out except for the few who had met us on arrival in Riga.

I was also keen to learn whether the vitriolic anti-Semitism of the war years had survived and, if so, what was being done about it. The information I got yielded no joy. Anti-Semitism, though muted, was still present. The government was ambivalent about the past and silent about the present.

It was now time to make a visit to the graves. After all, this was one of the key purposes of our journey. It transpired that this could only be organized for the next day so we adjourned to the one hotel in the town, where rooms had been reserved for us.

By world standards this would be classified as a one-star establishment, but it was large and fairly comfortable and we were satisfactorily installed and rested before sallying forth again into the streets. As time was short, we were pressured to see as much as possible that day.

First we went to the municipality to find out if we could receive compensation for our lost property and business. We were also interested in a rumour we had heard about the intention of the Latvian Government to pay compensation to war victims. It was not long before we were sitting in the office of a very efficient and courteous official who very quickly obtained from the archive all the documents necessary to answer our questions. To our amazement he had in front of him the entire record of the family's business. He told us exactly when my grandfather made his acquisition, what had been paid, what the turnover had been and on precisely what date the Russians had nationalized it. No compensation could be considered, because it was not the Latvians but the Russians who had instigated the nationalization. As for the house, it had been destroyed by fire during severe bombing and the ruins had been incorporated into a municipal park, thus ceasing to exist. We were given forms on which to request consideration for compensation.

That behind us, we ventured again into the streets in search of landmark buildings and places that had formed the setting for my childhood memories. To Diana's and Karen's surprise, I was able to point out and identify much that surrounded us. I must admit, though, that some of the buildings that I recollected as large were actually quite small. However, my school was still as impressive as it was when I was a child.

The sadness was quite overwhelming as we walked down street after street and I was able to identify many of the buildings linked to experiences that took place in my early years. The constant refrain was: 'here lived so-and-so – killed; here lived cousin Masha – killed.'

We now returned to the school for a final walk. I wanted to cover the daily stroll I used to experience with Masha, from the school back to our neighbourhood and home. We moved down the blocks that were easy to follow. They suddenly petered out against a grass bank where, from the distance, we had seen a green open space looming. Beyond lay a large landscaped park. This whole section, so intimately bound up with my early life, had obviously been the area where a concentration of bombs had fallen – as explained by the municipal official. I could not even identify the approximate spot where my home had stood.

Later we were able to contact my Nanny's niece and her son who lived in the nearby town of Kraslava. They came to see us at the hotel. After settling down, questions and answers followed rapidly. By this means we were able to pick up the precious lost threads and to understand the difficult lives these good people live. At least we were relieved to learn that my saintly Nanny survived for many years in some comfort.

To complete our day's programme, Sioma drove us out to the resort town of Stropi, where so many happy summer holidays had been spent. The lovely lake and beautiful forest is still there but we were saddened by the dilapidation that had been allowed to occur. Most of the dachas were constructed of wood and clearly most of the owners had not been able to afford the essential maintenance. Some of the older buildings had even been demolished. Nearby stood a few large factories that had very unwisely been allowed to build there in the intervening years. What shocked us was the magnitude of growth. In my childhood years the bus journey out took nearly an hour but now it is almost part of the spreading town.

On the return journey we passed the site of the prison where most of the men, including my father, had been so brutally incarcerated during the first days of occupation. The red-brick building I remembered was still standing. Across the road was the open space called Railway Park, where the men were forced to dig their own graves before being killed. Battling with my emotions I asked Sioma to drive on without stopping.

That evening was spent with Fira Aronowitz who was one of the few who were sent to Siberia as children and managed to survive. It was pleasant to be together but the past was really our only bond. She was able to flesh out for us, and particularly for the girls, much of what I only vaguely remembered or had completely forgotten about those distant times.

The final day of our stay in Daugavpils dawned. The last and most painful journey started after a tense breakfast. The road to the forest graves took us past the ghetto. We stopped. My mind was a jumble of memories. Karen and Diana gazed at the building with masked emotion. We had been told that the complex was now used as a prison for habitual criminals. After a few more minutes of poignant silence, Sioma drove on.

Next on the way was the Citadel. It was from there that the tattered and broken remnants of our community were taken on that nightmare journey to Riga and Kaiserwald concentration camp. Because of the significance of this enclave in the history of Latvia, schoolchildren were often brought here. Such a group happened to be present and were attentively gathered around their teacher.

We stopped and got out of the car in the hope of being allowed in. At the entrance we learnt that the Russian Army were still in occupation. We turned away and I must admit that I was relieved. For me this ancient precinct would have been a painful reliving of those lurking nightmares. We returned to the car. On the way we passed the group of schoolchildren again. On an impulse I greeted the young blonde teacher and reminded her about the grim recent history of this landmark. She looked at me coldly and did not utter a word.

An Ultimage Pilgrimage

We proceeded with the last leg of the journey, deep into the forest. Each one of us was lost in thought. The silence said it all. On either side of the twisting tarmac road the gloom of the trees pressed in on us. The sense of foreboding was palpable. At last we reached a clearing and Sioma stopped the car. Beyond was an open space the size of a small sports field, covered with small stones and divided into sections. Each was marked by a metal plaque with an identical inscription, but on each the number of Jews buried was acknowledged thus: 'Here lie 5,000 Jews who were killed'; 'Here lie 3,000 Jews who were killed'; 'Here lie 1,000 Jews who were killed.' And so on, around the clearing. Here and there a stark, unlettered stone-monument had been erected.

I stood there mute, reliving the horrors of the selections and seeing the thousands of women, children and men going to their deaths with no one to mourn them. Most of the killings took place in the forest so none would hear or see.

It is eerie to note that a strange phenomenon occurred here. All the communal graves had been covered with the original sand of the forest round about. For 50 years not a blade of grass had grown back anywhere. Scientists could not explain this strangeness. It was finally decided to cover the graves with small black and red marble chips but to this day they are different to similar graves elsewhere in Latvia, which are lush and green. I felt drained and numb. None of us had anything to say. No tear flowed. No birds flew. Not even the wind contributed a sigh.

Our pilgrimage was over.

We left my home town with bittersweet and terrible memories. Life there continued very much as before. The only real difference was that after hundreds of years of struggle, endeavour and achievement, there was no longer a viable Jewish community in existence. Race hatred had prevailed and inevitably tragedy and death had followed. But the land of my birth, much the poorer and, for me, much the sadder, had survived.

A Daughter's Comment

It was to be an adventure like no other – an adventure into a world of memories, ghosts, pain and suffering – but above all, an adventure led by a **survivor** of the Holocaust.

I had read my mother's early manuscript many years before. It was a documentary of her idyllic childhood in Dvinsk with my dearly beloved grandmother Rebecca, of blessed memory, and a grandfather, whom I never met; her dreams and aspirations in a setting of folk heroes – *babushkas* (grandmothers) in their floral shawls, balmy days drinking tea from the samovar at the dacha during the summer, the sound of sleigh bells and puffing horses like ghosts in the snow of winter. All this and more – 'till the Germans came.'

My sister Karen and I relived all these emotions from the magical scenes to the tragedy and horror of the Holocaust, on our visit to our mother's hometown of Dvinsk, in July 1992. It was her first time back 'home' after 50 years. We were filled with anticipation – not knowing what to expect and how she, or for that matter we, would react on such an emotional pilgrimage.

From the moment we set foot in Dvinsk (Daugavpils) the roles were reversed. Karen and I were the 'parents', providing words of reassurance and compassion, and our beloved mother, Maja, was a child once again. We were taken on a sightseeing tour of the town by an excited child whose early memories were filled with happiness. We passed the old Hebrew school, the dentist's rooms, the park where she tipped over in her pram, her father's shop, her cousin's house, the church she frequented (unbeknown to her parents) with her beloved Nanny, the station, the apartments of friends – all these were photographed and treasured as are the memories of happy times shared.

Not photographed and recorded but images lost for ever,

A Daughter's Comment

however, are her home and the synagogue – burnt to a cinder when the Germans set fire to the city.

So graphic were her stories of the time when she was incarcerated, that we could see the flames leap before our eyes and smell the fumes: so began our journey into hell with our mother – a hell we had heard about since our childhood, read about, but somehow could never put into context. Here we were being led through all the painful memories by an actual survivor – our mother.

Karen and I often remarked during this tour, on the unreality of the situation – 'is this really true?' The eeriness of the white nights seemed to extend out daylight viewing time – as if nothing was to be missed on this unique adventure.

We were shown the ghetto, the Citadel, the square where the men were rounded up and shot, the prison where our grandfather was held captive, the forests where graves were dug by the Jews for their own burial, the curt memorial plaques, the acres of barren earth covered by gravel stones because nothing will grow there – on the acres of graves of dead loved ones.

I remember picking up three gravel stones as a memento – these are a tangible memory of the horrors that she relived for us.

How could anyone have survived the living hell that she shared with us, not only here in her home town, but also in Riga, where she took us to the ghetto – a series of barracks – isolated from the town, eerie, uninhabited and depressing. We also visited the barren site of Kaiserwald, where her vivid description of the structures and her stories of the time incarcerated there seemed to recreate, in front of our eyes, the very camp in all its horror.

The few survivors still living in Riga became the lead players in this unfolding drama – Sioma Spungin, the childhood friend; Sara Rosenberg, the fellow ballerina; and Fira Aronowitz, the survivor from Siberia – all filled us with emotion at this 'once in a lifetime' meeting.

After our fond but sad farewells, we left this world of voices crying out in the night, the ghosts of the past and the shared experiences, full of awe and admiration for our grandmother Rebecca, our mother Maja, and the few surviving friends.

To Forgive...But Not Forget

Above all, we kept reminding ourselves of our privilege – to be the children of a survivor, and to have shared the real images of the past with her, as observers and comforters – to be part of her world, as it was, even long before we were born.

Diana Judith Smullen (neé Abramowitch)
December 1998

Reverie

As I sit in my beautiful house or in the peace of my garden, I find myself becoming increasingly introspective. As my mind drifts back, I find it difficult to differentiate between what was a dream and what was reality.

My present life being so different in comparison, I often wonder if the horrors of the past did happen; did the Holocaust, in fact, take place, did I really go back again – or is it just a nightmare or dream from which I will soon awaken?

But what of the nightmare that is in fact a reality that one cannot shake off – a reality so terrifying that one hopes and continues to hope that it is only a nightmare? What of the reality that is so grim that one cannot in all sanity accept it, because one cannot believe that humans can possibly do such hideous and inhuman things to men, women and children?

How does one come out of such ordeals? Unscathed? Hardly! Whilst enjoying the comforts that life has now generously bestowed on me, at times pain assails me at the thought of throwing away even a piece of bread or a strand of string... No, the past structures the present and to forget is to damn tomorrow.

Postscript

This is the story of the greatest tragedy the world has known. The story of genocide, where all civilized standards of compassion, social conscience and common decency were subjugated to brutal, pitiless prejudice and cruelty.

It is also the story of courage and faith and the will to live by ordinary decent folk who desire nothing from life but fair play and human kindness. It is a story simply told, without bitterness on the one hand or exaggeration on the other, but with a profound humility and thankfulness for the occasional exhibitions of people's better selves.

This story, told by Maja Abramovitch, is factual, and relates her experiences and those of her mother during the Holocaust of the Second World War.

In this particular case, the villains of the piece were the Germans under Hitler. The lesson to be learnt is that Germans are not the only people who can be blinded by propaganda and prejudice. There are very few countries in both the West and the East where such events are not possible. It has happened in the 'Free' African countries without exception, and in Europe and Asia. South Africans are only too conscious of the exaggerated prejudice of people who should know better.

Maja Abramovitch has experienced what happens when innocent people are the victims of manic hatred and ignorance. It did happen. Let the world stop, look and listen, and not allow it to happen again.

Dr Jack Penn

Epilogue

In these pages I have recalled for posterity the progression of my life from a wonderful, secure, almost dreamlike childhood, to four years of the most inhuman nightmare that mankind has known. It is my fervent hope that knowledge of these events can help prevent their ever happening again. I am aware, however, that individual experiences such as mine, once recorded, are most unlikely to join the body of currently available literature in moving public opinion against the scourge of race hatred.

To contribute to an effective awareness of the destructive forces of racism on nations, it is necessary to combat bigotry, prejudice and intolerance, which are its basic ingredients. To do this effectively, I believe it is necessary to start with active school programmes at an early age. These will teach fundamental values of decency and goodness, the attributes that form an integral part of all religions based on the directives of the Almighty. It is necessary to ensure that these values become a natural part of daily living and to show how their critical absence in the hideous philosophies of the racists resulted in the inevitability of the Holocaust.

I have struggled hard to overcome, in myself, a hatred of those who cruelly destroyed my early life and my family and almost succeeded in exterminating my people. Having now completely overcome my disturbing initial reactions, I have come to realize that there are no basically evil nations or racial groups in the world. There are only evil people, mostly seekers after wealth or power, who will utilize any aberration of the human mind, no matter how base, dishonest, or distorted, to achieve their devilish ends. An examination of Bosnia, Russia and Rwanda will yield good examples.

In essence, the story of that part of my life recorded here is one of caring love and depraved hatred. I have spent the greater part of my life contemplating the presence of both scenarios as important components of human life. The power of caring love leads to all the wondrous miracles of a beautiful life. Hatred only leads to tragedy and disaster. In a world not of dreams but of stark reality the only essential meaning of life can be found in the scenario of the former. That scenario can only happen if the people of all nations intensely and practically will it so.

Appendix 1: Footnotes of History

1933–41

In 1933 Hitler, through treachery and intrigue, became the dictator of Germany. The stage was set for events that would eventually give rise to the Second World War and the devastation of Europe.

After signing a Non-Aggression Pact with the Soviet Union on 25 August 1939, the way was open for the attack on Poland by Germany, on 1 September 1939. In the terms of the pact the Russians were free to invade Lithuania, Latvia and Estonia, as well as Eastern Poland.

In fact the Non-Aggression Pact was a ploy to buy time for the defeat of France and Great Britain while adding the capture of Belgium, Holland, Denmark and Norway in the sweep of the victorious German forces.

Having secured most of these various military objectives, Hitler informed his generals that the next goal was to wipe out Russia's very existence. Operation Barbarossa, the code name for the invasion of Russia, was launched on the 22 June 1944. The trap was sprung. One of the greatest slaughters mankind has known was the result.

1943

On 31 January 1943 the German invasion of Russia suffered a mortal blow. After ferocious battles the invaders were halted at Stalingrad where General Paulus surrendered with the remnant of his stricken forces. From that time on the general retreat westwards began. In spite of great suffering, some battles were still being won by the invading forces, but the virtually irresistible build-up of Soviet armed might could not be withstood by the the now demoralized invaders.

To Forgive... But Not Forget

In May 1943 the German forces in Africa were finally defeated by the combined forces of the British Commonwealth and the United States. The Allies then moved their offensive to Sicily and Italy and planned the liberation of the rest of mainland Europe. The U-boat menace, which had threatened to throttle the Allied war effort up to the middle of 1943, was slowly being overcome. Food, men and war material were once again starting to flow from America to reinforce the Allied struggle against Germany.

At this time the Russian war effort was also being strengthened by the arrival of 'lend-lease' tanks, aircraft and other much-needed resources. This assistance hastened the formation of new fighting groups and strengthened the indomitable spirit of the beseiged civilians. Through the summer and autumn of 1943, following on the defeat of the German 6th Army at Stalingrad, the mounting momentum of the Russian counter-offensive was beginning to push back the invading forces.

By August the Russians were crashing through to the Ukraine and beyond. Pressures from the Allied invasion of Italy necessitated a transfer of some much-needed German troop reinforcements to southern Europe. The resultant weakening of the enemy's front in the East assisted the Russian advance towards the areas of Europe where the infamous death camps had long been established.

1944

By January 1944 the Russians, who had already recaptured Kiev – the capital of the Ukraine – began their push towards Poland and the Baltic States. The invasion of Germany and the capture of Berlin was their objective.

On 6 June 1944 the Allied invasion of France began. After hard-fought battles, Paris was captured on 26 August. The Soviet spring offensive of that year had carried the victorious Russian Army to the outskirts of the Polish capital, Warsaw. East Prussia was threatened. By the end of 1944 the advance overran Estonia, Latvia and Lithuania. By the beginning of 1945 virtually all of Europe with the exception of Germany itself had been captured – by the Allies, from the West and the Russians, from the East.

Appendix 1: Footnotes of History

1945

In January 1945 the final advance on a beleaguered Germany began. The Allies struck from the west across the river Rhine. The Russians struck from the north and southwest. After frightful battles marked by intense bravery, sacrifice and bloodshed, April heralded the beginning of the end. On 7 May 1945 the exhausted victors and broken vanquished signed the final surrender documents.

Appendix 2: Monuments

In a brochure I received from Riga around 1980, it seems that Latvia can pride itself on having hosted 23 concentration camps during the German occupation.

At the seventeenth milestone on the main road between Riga and Dvinsk (Daugavpils) was Salaspils, the largest of the camps. Now there is a beautiful park in its place, with sculptures and monuments erected to commemorate the dead. This is, in fact, the only place where tourists are taken and where, once a year, a memorial service for the dead is held. The authorities do not encourage remembering. Nowhere on the monuments is it mentioned that Jews died there. On a big stone that stands on the place where the victims were hanged, the inscription reads:

HERE INNOCENT PEOPLE WERE EXECUTED BECAUSE THEY WERE INNOCENT. HERE PEOPLE WERE EXECUTED BECAUSE EACH ONE OF THEM WAS HUMAN AND LOVED HIS HOMELAND.

Yet Jews from Austria, Germany, Czechoslovakia, Poland, Hungary – and other places – were brought here to be killed. I would say that 90 per cent of the Latvian Jews were destroyed in Latvia, yet in only one place in the whole brochure are the Jews mentioned, and then only to say that of the 600,000 people killed in the camps, the overwhelming majority were Jews.

Of the few other monuments erected in Russia to point out the mass graves, the Jewish victims are included only under the banner of 'Soviet Citizens'.

Maja Abramowitch
February 1995

Glossary

Afikomen	a piece of matzo that the head of the family hides; the children find it, but do not return it to the father until he has paid a forfeit
Aktion	the violent procedure of selecting Jews destined for the death process
Amcho	'of your people'
Angros	wholesaler
Appell	roll call
Babushka	grandmother
Bedsedka	summerhouse
Bloodwors	sausage
Dacha	house in the country
Dvornik	yardman
Haggadah	the story of the Jews exile from Egypt
Hanukkah	the Festival of Lights
Isargs	Latvian Fascists
Judenrat	council of the Jews
Kapo	Overseer (usually a camp inmate appointed by the Germans)
Kneidlach	matzo balls
Kommando	a work party
Kristallnacht	'Night of the Broken Glass': anti-Semitic pogrom in Germany, November 1938
Matric	examination
Matzo(s)	Unleavened bread eaten during Pesach
Nachschlag	second helping
Obersturmführer	1st lieutenant in the SS
Pesach	Passover
Pilaff	

Pioneers	Junior Communist League
Politruks	political instructors
Seder	communal/family dinner on the eve of Pesach
Shein	work permit
Shoah	the Holocaust
Succah	traditional festive eating booths
Succoth	Feast of Tabernacles
Talmud	Rabbinic commentary on the Old Testament
Valinki	high felt boots
Vedma	witch
Yekkes	a term for German Jews used by camp inmates
Yom Kippur	Day of Atonement